DR. PARM

Flourishing
Relationships

PURAN HOYE CHITT KI ICHA

Understanding, seeking
and finding your heart's desire

Cover by Gurpreet Singh Sahota
Illustrations by Tjader Anderson

ISBN 978-1-913663-42-1

Printed in Great Britain by
Biddles Books Limited, King's Lynn, Norfolk

Contents

Dedication

How many times have you found something you are looking for right under your nose? After a lot of personal struggles, I found out this is true for love, happiness and contentment. The problem is that we choose instead to seek beyond ourselves for the very things with which we are naturally bestowed. Life then become more challenging than it should be.

Somewhere along the journey of life, I lost my sense of being-*ness* and fell asleep at the steering wheel. Finally, and inevitably, my journey ended in a crash – a heart attack – nearly losing my life. "Life has delivered a blow to poor old me," I thought. But it was quite the opposite.

I had been given a second chance of life - to find under my nose the very things I had been desperately seeking. And I found them through relationships that had always surrounded and supported me, no matter what. It is was through them I began to see and know myself again. Relationships are some of the most effective ways of flourishing in life, because you are 'really there' for each other.

To finally say *"puran hoye chitt ki Icha"* – all that I sought has been fulfilled – and to finally live as a human *being*.

I wish to dedicate this book to my wife, children, friends, relatives and colleagues, who have always supported and believed in me. And for those with whom, for whatever reason, I didn't see eye-to-eye, I thank you, too – for, without you, I wouldn't be who I am today.

Parminder Singh

Introduction

Gursharan, my wife, and I often talk about the day's events, or reflect on the week when winding down and settling in for the night. This week she told me about how, when watching a television soap which she enjoys, she had felt a strong emotional reaction to the storyline. She feels more easily touched by events around her than I do.

It was interesting that she wanted to mention this specifically to me. I listened to her telling me how relatively simple events between people can deeply move her, sometimes to tears.

I became quite emotional with the realisation that, after 41 years of marriage (this year), we still communicate freely, share our feelings and thoughts and support each other in every possible way, no matter what is thrown into our paths. When I had gathered myself, I told her that I loved her and that the whole family loved her. We all have each other. We should enjoy the love and use it to be fearless in our journey together.

Our relationship has been, and is, a gift of life for me. I know she feels the same, but it hasn't always been easy for her. I hadn't realised how badly I had treated her until I was provided – not out of choice – with an opportunity to re-examine my life. On a hot summer's day in June 1996, at the age of only 39 and after only 18 years of marriage, I was diagnosed with critical heart failure.

As I was being advised by the doctors, in the emergency room at the hospital, that I had suffered an acute heart attack, I looked towards my wife for support and comfort. She was at my bedside, holding my hand. I felt lost and scared. This was new territory for me and I associated it with the end for me.

Just for a moment, I saw fear in her eyes, too. In an instant, she composed herself. She gently squeezed my hand and said, "I am here for you." With that, she gave me the courage to accept what had happened and hope for my recovery. Just words cannot do that. They were her words. I knew her as a rock. All that she was came out of those words, that gesture and her presence by my side. This is the power of relationships. When you believe in what somebody does and has done for you, their love, the God in them, lifts you from despair into hope.

Stephen Covey, in his book *The 7 Habits of Highly Effective People* distinguishes between 'proactive' people - those who take responsibilities of their own lives and focus their efforts on things which they can do something about - and 'reactive' people, who abdicate responsibility and blame, accuse, behave like victims, pick on other people's weaknesses and complain about external factors over which they have no control. I felt Gursharan with me on this 'proactive' journey.

Gradually, with the support of my wife and children, I learnt to accept the change in my life situation. The solutions to my physical health lay, pretty much, in the hands of medical professionals.

In spite of myself, I slowly became aware that the speed of recovery and quality of my life also depended on the state of my mind. This aspect of my recovery was not clear to me in the beginning. I had a lot of time on my hands in the hospital and, as if guided by a mysterious hand, I began to reflect on the life I had led.

I gradually began to feel disappointment and shame at the difference between living as part of a family and living to control others and have them serve me. How did I let myself become so narcissistic?

As I lay sick on my hospital bed, my thoughts went first to the person who was constantly by my bedside, encouraging and comforting me to get better. I saw the pain and worry in her eyes. We had three young children and had emigrated to the UK only a few weeks earlier. I could feel the burden of uncertainty and worry on her shoulders.

My thoughts drifted back to our relationship. The first few years of our marriage had been magical. We were both carefree, happy and full of laughter and promise. In later years, the pressures of an expanding family business and misguided priorities took their toll on our relationship. I simply took out all my failings and frustrations on her.

I had let my wife down countless times, and in many ways. Taking her for granted, drunken cries for sympathy for previous 'lost loves' and not contributing to the daily needs of a growing family. She did her very best to give us all a chance of a future. This is despite having to withstand the pressures of living as part of an extended family.

It feels a terrible, hurtful and cruel thing to put somebody through! I was not proud of myself and, even to this day, the regret keeps me vigilant about taking care of those I love. Taking care to 'put my best being forward,' as Jordan Peterson, the Canadian psychologist, calls it.

Everyone who knew me thought of me as a loving, caring and compassionate person. Yet, hidden away from the world, another part of me was ugly and cruel.

As I became busier with work, I had time for little else. My business was my life compass, purpose and reward. Relationships with my wife and children were built on an arrogant attitude based around exerting control and giving instruction. "I know what is best for us," and "Toe the line or else," was my expectation, and my wife and children had no choice but to "conform" to my demands. I kept them "happy" with the comforts which money could buy, I rationalised. I was a good person and worked hard to look after my family, I reasoned. In reality, I was limiting the lives of those I love. They felt the torment that I disguised as care and duty.

Had I really become that evil? I have read somewhere that evil never looks like evil, and disguises itself as good. Interestingly the word Lucifer, a term usually used to refer to the devil – the personification of evil - actually means the light-bearer.

My thoughts exposed deeper concerns about the difference between my intentions and claims about myself, and the person who was visible through my actions. Was I a narcissist? Are you born as a narcissist, or become one later on in life, I asked myself Had I afflicted my relationship with deceit, manipulation, and emotional sabotage? Was my love like a lasso that got tighter and tighter every day? Little by little, making those around me lose their identity, will, and even their voice?

I had read somewhere that narcissists, despite their seemingly strong personality, are vulnerable underneath their protective armour. That is why command of their feelings and other people is all-important. They feel weak and humiliated without some sort of hold or control.

Or had I become egocentric – full of arrogance, ambition and, perhaps exhibitionism? I am told that people with this type of personality tend to think they're the most important person in the room, and that all eyes should be on them at all times.

People who couldn't care less about other people's opinions and focus only on their own are egocentric. Perhaps self-centred, too - only seeing the world from my point of view. Had I lost the ability to empathise and care about the consequences of my actions?

While I could identify with some of these characteristics, I took some comfort in the fact that these had only manifested to some degree in the last few years of my life. I had to remind myself that, apart from the last few years, my life had been full of laughter, joy and an easy manner. I had always been a caring individual who was easily moved to tears of pain or joy. I pondered on what could have brought on this (temporary) insanity. The only plausible explanation I could come up with was that I had been overwhelmed by the responsibilities I had inadvertently taken on, not only for my own wife and children, but also for the extended family. Added to this mix was the fact that my father and three brothers worked in the same business.

The long and short of it all was that, as the business and families expanded, I had felt overwhelmed because I didn't have the skills to manage such a mix of challenges.

I certainly felt, on reflection, a sense of doom and despair that my life was not mine any more, and that there was no escape from the quagmire of relationships that I felt trapped in. It was self-imprisonment, I admitted to myself. I finally concluded that my actions and behaviour, while in no way excusable, arose from the fact that I felt a sense of helplessness and hopelessness. Trapped, I could see no way of defending myself from the world, either emotionally or physically. The only thing I could do was lash out at the people who loved me, and whom I should have cared for in the first instance. That should have been my priority.

But, in spite of all this, Gursharan chose to hang around – and I am forever grateful that she did.

I also tried to figure out why she chose to stay in such a toxic relationship. Perhaps she had become convinced that she should be grateful for any smidgen of caring I provided on rare occasions. Or was it a fear of financial instability (I seriously doubt this), or just staying put because of our children?

But trying to stay together for the children isn't the best thing for the children, either, and definitely not the best thing for either partner. A bad relationship between parents often affects the children just as much as it impacts the parents.

Or did she put up with my nonsense because of what had happened to her in the past? In part, I knew, she, being the eldest in her family, felt a responsibility for the wellbeing of her own family, too.

She had lost her father at a young age and, being the eldest, saw herself as a role model to her four siblings. She probably didn't want to pile more pressure of her own problems on to the other many challenges that her widowed mother faced.

In Indian culture, there is stigma attached to divorce. There is a fear of what one's actions might have on the welfare of other family members. Perhaps she thought that, if she walked out of the marriage, her family's name could be tarnished – despite the fact that it was my stupidity.

I have asked her these very questions many times. Her answer is simply that she always looks at the bigger picture, and does not dwell on the negatives or the past. Everything comes to pass, and her attitude is always to face the present situation with a clarity of thought that is not influenced by the emotions of the moment.

I suspect her "seeing bigger picture" includes all the nuances of family, divorce, children, growing up without a father and my (temporary) insanity. She describes her motto of life simply as "just get on with it!" Don't get me wrong – she can get really emotional, but it takes a lot of pushing and shoving to get her to that tipping-point! If she tips, I get out of the way and go for a long – a very long - walk.

Most importantly, and I desperately cling to this, the reason she stuck around is that she loved me and could see beyond my shortcomings, and also see the potential I had for becoming a good husband and father. But, deep down, I feel with a sense of certainty that she understood what I was going through and that she, too, felt the same sense of responsibility to my family as I did.

I am reminded of Merrit Malloy's poem *The People Who Didn't Say Goodbye,* in which she speaks about people who never say goodbye – "... they are keepers of promises/what moves them does not wear them out. Their loyalty will tear apart your clocks...."

What do these people have inside them to make them this way? I know what my wife has. She has the ability to look beyond frailty, and has an unshakeable belief that, given the opportunity, we are all capable of being better human beings.

To be honest, it is the only thing that keeps me sane. But we cannot keep on beating ourselves up if we want to learn from our mistakes, make amends and move on to a better life. Especially if we have been given a second chance.

I take comfort from this wonderful advice from the *Book of Life* – "We may be experts at beating ourselves up, but this is a banal sport we've triumphed at for too long. Let's try exploring the forgotten glamour of giving ourselves a break and, once in a while, of turning towards light, reassurance, and a bit of compassionate cosiness." Excellent advice!

My thoughts continued. Lying by yourself, unable to take care of yourself without assistance, tends to focus the mind. I could gradually see more clearly what was required. What action I needed to take so that my living could be a force for good.

Most of us, at some point in our lives, start reading or listening to motivational materials whilst seeking answers to life's questions. Eckart Tolle, the author of *The Power of Now,* was one of the many I turned to. One of his teachings provided a pathway for me to consider and follow.

He calls it "alert presence". He advises you to single out this moment from the situation you find yourself in, and then your focal point is not in the life situation, but the present moment – not clouded by other emotions. Then true change is possible and, sometimes, change can happen without you doing anything.

This struck a note with me. I had to rise above the emotions that come with a life-threatening situation and make both the mental and physical recoveries my focal point. As I began the process of healing, my first thoughts were about the care and love I was receiving, not only from my family and friends, but from total strangers, too.

All of us are surrounded by different types of relation- ships. They serve their purpose. Some are transient and others endure. Ultimately, all relationships involve a contribution from us and a response to us. Thus, they become reflections of us. Careful, though; we see what we want to see, or have the ability to see. The same rock can be a building-stone for the future, or a window into history. It depends upon our perspective. How badly do you really want to know?

The first lesson that I had learnt was that the relationship which we have with ourselves is the one that we should long for. Who and what are we? Others guide us. We see ourselves in their struggles, hopes, dreams, successes. We see ourselves through what they reflect back to us.

This is partly what is meant by 'finding yourself'. Understanding what has made you as you are. What do you really wish for? What do you want to be?

The most time we spend is with ourselves; even when we are surrounded by people, we are still with ourselves. What must it be like not to know who we are with? Any relationship begins and ends with how well we intimately understand ourselves.

What are our likes and dislikes? What do we want, or need, from others, and what can we offer them? We should not hesitate to share who and what we really are with the people we love.

By knowing ourselves better, we can understand others better. We recognise qualities in others, because they are familiar to us from within. How else would we recognise compassion, for example? There must be compassion within us already. With a deeper knowledge of ourselves, our relationships with others will be more engaging, bringing us joy and fulfilment.

We need this understanding and personal mastery about ourselves to be able to commit to a relationship in a conscious way. Otherwise our relationships, including the one with ourselves, will be mostly superficial games of entertainment. According to Dr Marta Wilson, an internationally-recognized speaker, people who are personally masterful manage their minds, bodies and spirits. They take responsibility for the results they achieve. They hold a proper attitude for learning new things. They see their connection to everything around them, including when things go right and when things go wrong. They remain focused and prepared for every life event. People with personal mastery inspire change, welcome change, foster change and sustain change — change in themselves.

The process of personal mastery forces us to do what most people have a very hard time doing – assessing ourselves as more than the sum of a list of faults. As our focus broadens, the accuracy of our self-assessment improves. In addition to our talents and strengths, we identify opportunities for growth. But, in the context of personal mastery, some weaknesses turn out to be nothing more than strengths that have not been fully developed. The question is not how to get rid of them, but how to harness their full power.

Personal mastery, she adds, is the differentiating variable in determining individual success. For success, personal mastery must become a way of life. Personal mastery is an evolutionary process, beginning at our core with productive solitude full of reflection and honesty. There, we become more and more conscious of ourselves as leaders – and as individuals. As we make conscious choices to evolve and to embrace change, we become freer to respond with clarity, commitment and energy to the circumstances around us – they have an impact on us, and we on them.

This book is about developing personal mastery, of understanding, seeking and finding your heart's desire. It's about the value of relationships and knowing yourself better because of others. It's about initiating, developing and sustaining relationships.

All different in purpose and experience but, ultimately, all helping you experience the world, yourself and, sometimes, as the Lebanese-American writer and poet Khalil Gibran said, having "the winds of heaven dance between you."

Seeing yourself and your relationships as they are, instead of seeing them as imagined, is important. Knowing yourself enables you to make conscious choices in the types of relationship you have, or choose to have in the future.

Based on personal experiences and stories, each chapter in this book is a meditation on a journey that begins with a transformational incident that precipitates a journey of deeper self-discovery.

Chapter 1: Facing Myself

This chapter leads us to understand the truth about ourselves, no matter how painful it is to face. Recognise the darker side of yourself and your potential for mayhem, as well as your contribution to joy around you. Understand how you use these to be a beacon for your purpose in life. When you do that, you are attracted and sensitised to people and experiences that let you be yourself, as you are when you feel at home. Home is where we can be ourselves. Not obliged to meet social norms, or imagined cultural expectations. That is what freedom feels like. Being and doing what comes naturally to us.

Home is a wonderful breath of release of what is not you, and an embracing of what you are. This is where we long to be, how we want to exist and, sometimes, we can feel this way with somebody we meet. That we can feel at home in somebody's company is a great sign of a healthy relationship.

Chapter 2: Seeking Forgiveness and Reconciliation

This chapter begins by deconstructing my messed-up life. Everything is simpler when it is deconstructed. I was done with peering at life through a highly-distorted lens.

We get addicted to the way we choose to live. It is difficult to stop being an addict, because the person experiencing it – and others – may not recognize it as destructive, compulsive behaviour. My addiction was a mindset – a belief system based on excuses and justifications that said 'my happiness is somewhere out there, not right here' – in a substance, in a relationship, in an amount of money in my bank account. My mindset had to change. My framework for living re-examined.

Finally, it looks at how reconciliation is as important as forgiveness. I wanted not only to be forgiven, but also to find a way to restore these fractured relationships to some extent. Reconciliation within myself was equally important. It was part of the process of self-forgiveness. Forgiveness and wellbeing are closely linked. Remembering times when life was good also provided me with the belief that I could experience joy again. To discover myself again, so that I can share myself with those I love.

Chapter 3: Finding Meaning in My Suffering

In this chapter I had to face my suffering head-on, and didn't want this trauma to become overwhelming. I had to be careful not to get caught up in self-pity and feelings of hopelessness and worthlessness. I had to properly understand, process or move on from it and, without fear, prepare myself to build a better, brighter future in which I was an active participant in my relationships.

The chapter explores how relationships give us the gifts of companionship, intimacy, support and challenge. They also reflect back onto us... so that we can better know who we are. Relationships can support us and give us guidance and courage to step into uncertainty and find meaning through our experiences, be they suffering or exhilaration.

Chapter 4: Rewriting My Own Story

I wanted my life to change, and was tired of being in a rut, tired and confused. How could I break out of this cycle of, ultimately, self-destruction?

Sick and tired of abusing and abandoning myself, I wanted to participate in life so that I could live for myself, and my loved ones, in feelings of peace and happiness. II wanted the opportunity to rewrite my story on my own terms, without concern for imaginary expectations that did not really have any bearing on my life.

I wanted to develop and pursue the talents I was born with and, perhaps, destined for; I wanted to be "in my element" and use my near-death experience as a springboard to re-discover and follow my heart's desire. (In Gurmukhi, my language from birth - *Puran Hoye Chitt ki Icha*.)

Chapter 5: Moving Towards What Matters Most

Fear can prevent us from doing things that we truly want to do. We can either choose to succumb to bitterness, disillusionment, resentment and depression, or learn to forgive and heal ourselves by identifying and facing our fears and developing self-compassion. Through that, we can begin to reclaim our natural selves. Follow our *Chitt ki Icha*.

Before we can support others, we need to support ourselves, through self-compassion. We can then create a secure base, an anchor, to stabilise and steer us through challenges. Self-compassion is an essential part of being well emotionally, psychologically, relationally, physically and even spiritually.

This chapter is about how self-compassion can help us to have the motivation and the courage to engage in behavioural changes, leading us to live bigger lives, and move towards what and who matter most to us.

Chapter 6: Conscious Living

Once we develop conscious awareness, we can make more careful choices. We can then choose how to live, rather than react to events and people we meet. Page xxi Responding from our character traits includes gratitude, contentment, patience and appreciation, rather than our cultivated personality. Responding from our virtues rather that morals.

The single biggest impediment to happiness and fulfilment results from an impaired awareness. Many people scurry about their daily lives absorbed in their thoughts, processing memories of pain and regret, or expecting a future they wish for to arrive by default. By becoming more conscious in our everyday living, we can use our desires, needs and ambitions to move from this moment to the next. Making these choices based upon the conditioning of our automatic and reactive living will not lead to change.

Everybody has choices and makes decisions, but not always skilfully. Understand what you are choosing.

Its source, substance and consequence. If somebody upsets you, look at the person, not just the behaviour. Discernment taught me the consequences of choosing wrongly, of being attracted by meaningless things, of being seduced by others, or being trapped in relationships.

Chapter 7: Relationships As Gifts Of Love

Relationships give us the gift of love. How can this love be made visible, daily, and help us rise and live our best life possible? How can relationships serve – help – us in what we want to do, guide us to do things we need and sometimes in doing things that we did not even know we could do?

The secret lies in accepting the present moment as the richest apex of being. In the past, it fades away as memories and, in the future, as a series of aspirations. By keeping close to life, every moment is fresh. Your relationships keep fresh, born again and again and, in this way, become gifts of love.

In short, do it for the love of it. In love you learn to give. To give without condition, caveats and expectations is a true gift of love.

Chapter 8: Value Inner Beauty

This chapter is about going beyond the superficial and connecting with an inner beauty, characterised by unconditional love and kindness.

While our outer appearances change, our inner beauty lasts a lifetime. That is where our value lies, and that is how we can hold on to and have great relationships. I could now put my past behind me and acknowledge that the real essence of my being had never been lost. It had just become covered by layers of misjudgements, wrong decisions and the choice of wrong paths that had resulted in unbearable pain. Pain that had disguised itself as some sort of deluded personal achievement.

Stripped of all these delusions, I was still the same person who had a passion for life before getting waylaid. By freeing myself from these self-imagined and self-imposed burdens, I began to lose my sense of fear and become more courageous and open to explore experiences and opportunities as they presented themselves. My relationships began to have more meaning and become more natural, because now they arose from my heart and not the mind.

Chapter 9: One-ness

This chapter is about the realisation of the one-ness of life. It is the discovery and experiencing of the life as continuous flow, driven by intuition and spontaneity. It discusses the sense of connectedness and contentment that one experiences living in this way. It's being like the artist or musician in your relationships and avoiding deconstructing everything in order to label and measure.

It's when we go beyond structures in relationships that we feel the essence or substance of what they give to us. This leads to love. Romantic love, the love of friends, or just the love of our fellow human beings. It feels as if we have a shared being – a shared reality. We all long for this feeling of comfort, immersion or one-ness, just as we do when we get lost listening to music, or see a wonderful landscape or painting that takes us away from the events in our life to our pleasures, dreams and comforts of living.

I have now experienced first-hand how it feels not to be bottled up, to be spontaneous, to feel part of something bigger than me and just flow with whatever is happening in the moment. This is one-ness – going with the natural flow.

I hope that the journey of facing myself, rebuilding relationships and appreciating what I have rather than do not have, will at least make you pause and think about how your own relationships touch you and shape you. It is my hope that you live with yourself happily, because your relationships constantly help you understand why you love and are loved. I hope this gives you and those you love the freedom and courage to understand, seek, and find your heart's desire – *Puran Hoye Chitt ki Icha.*

Chapter 1

Facing Myself

This chapter is about letting go of expectations, wherever they come from, to re-connecting with the person you truly and naturally are. This will feel so comfortable, intuitive and easy, it will feel like coming home. Think about it; home is where we can be ourselves. We begin by facing truths about ourselves, no matter how painful and difficult they may be to accept. Here you will meet good and bad intentions, blindness to what is happening around you and behaviours that hurt others. You convince yourself that these behaviours give you comfort.

Now you will face the fact that it actually feeds your self-deceit. Once you discover and catch this darker, limiting and distorting side of yourself, your road to recovery can begin. To commit to being who you really are, you also have to promise to reject that which you have become. Then you have to deliver on your promise. If you do not make this change happen, you are destined to be blown by life's storms and eventually, when you are no use to others and they to you, bitterness and resentment will take over. You will have rejected the constant presence of love in favour of shooting stars - a life of momentary pleasures that, ultimately, leave you untouched and empty.

Home is comfort. A wonderful breath of release of what is not you, and an embracing of what you are. That is what freedom feels like, natural, genuine. Not obliged to meet social norms or imagined cultural expectations. Thriving because we are living to our natural desires and behaviours.

This is where we long to be, how we want to exist and, sometimes, we meet somebody who reflects back at us feelings and emotions that feel like home.

It may be a strong emotion or a faint glimmer of a smile. That is the outer light. It feels like your inner light. It feels like home. This is the start of that relationship. Light touching light. Home from home. From being me with me, to being me with you.

Finding our way back home is not easy. We collect a lot of baggage and get lost on the way. We have to let go, lighten our load, get rid of that which holds us back. But letting go is not easy.

When we are unable to let go, that works against us, holding us back. Instead of creating the future we are intuitively drawn to, we create one that makes the most of that which we have accumulated during our chase for, primarily, material and commercial success. As the Dalai Lama once said: "People were meant to be loved and materials to be used. We now live to love materials and use people." This leads to a dead end – literally.

So, what is your story? Your story is what you tell yourself to justify your decisions. You might tell yourself you can't have a successful relationship because of how you grew up. Or you might have picked a wrong career path that pays well, but is unfulfilling and causes you pain and stress. Or it might be failed relationships that you simple cannot let go.

Your personal story might include how you view yourself – perhaps low self-esteem or lack of confidence. Your story might include cultural and religious beliefs that lock you in a perpetual cycle of guilt and shame. It might also include what others think about you.

If you can't get out of the story you've constructed for yourself, then you cannot move on toward bigger and brighter things. Please let me share my story. A story that began to take shape a few years after my marriage, when I allowed myself to be plunged into a family business that not only ended with damaged individuals and relationships, but also emotional breakdown.

Page 3

It was 1977 and I had come back from the US A after completing both undergraduate and graduate studies. My father had moved heaven and earth to send me to the USA - it wasn't cheap, especially as I attended a private university, but he had had dreams and aspirations for me. My younger brother worked with him while I was studying. I was the first one from our community to achieve such a high level of education. I was full of confidence and pride. I had fulfilled a promise and was ready to make my mark in the world.

I remember clearly the day when I saw them for the first time upon my return. My father looked tired and worn-out, but his face lit up when he saw me. I could sense that he saw hope in the future now that I was back with knowledge and skills. My brother was replacing a gearbox on a truck. He looked different and all grown up. I was 17 when I left for university, so he must have been 15. So many years seemed to have flown by.

My mother had come to pick me up from the airport and all she could do was cry tears of joy. She was not one for complicating living. She called it as she saw it. My younger sisters and the youngest brother were just happy to see me.

My father had bought a new car for me and had employed a trained chef to cook for me. In typical Punjabi manner he reasoned, "My son has returned from America as an educated man. He must be used to eating western food. We – the whole family – must adjust to make him feel welcome."

I felt great, and accepted (graciously) this royal treatment. Little did they know I had lived almost like a hippy in the USA; come on, man, it was the 70s! Besides the academic education, I had also received, in the university dorms and weekend "excursions", insights and experiences which, if revealed (then), would have sent my parents to an early grave (well, we cremate, not bury our departed, but you get the gist of what I am saying).

The cook did not last more than a couple of weeks because, again in typical Punjabi manner, my mother kept on complaining that he was free most of the time and that he should also do other household chores, such as washing, sweeping, cleaning… and cook for the other family members, too!

The poor fellow had worked as a personal cook for ambassadors and diplomats, and was having none of this. He didn't show up at breakfast one morning, and I was left looking at what the rest of the siblings were having. It was a long way down and I landed with a thump, while my siblings had a good laugh – they used to say, again in Punjabi, "He has a big head and *akarr* (akarr in Punjabi means stiffness – being full of yourself).

Jokes aside, we were open and warm towards each other. There were no hidden meanings or intentions behind the emotions, and perhaps that is why it seemed so natural and right. We just knew we were there for each other and, no matter what was thrown our way, we would overcome it and we would be OK. Little did we realise the opposite would happen, and that some us would not even speak to each other after a few years.

A couple of weeks after I had settled back, and a few days after the cook had left, my father called me into his office to discuss work. He began by saying how proud he was of my achievements, and especially for maintaining my Sikh appearance. Next, he spoke about his dreams for the future. He saw me as taking over the family business, which consisted of a haulage company and two mechanical repair workshops.

I was so grateful for the sacrifices he had made for me, especially for my education, that I felt obliged to agree. This felt like subtle and skilful emotional blackmail but, at the back of my mind, I believed he had good intentions.

At the end of the day, I could have spoken out and said that this line of work was not for me. And we see this play out in all our relationships. We often say "yes" just to keep the peace, instead of speaking out and clearly expressing how we really feel. Otherwise, take it from me, it comes back to bite you, as it did for me.

Agreeing to work together was the beginning and end of my own personal dreams. I had wanted to work in the charity sector and carry out projects that benefited the less fortunate of our society.

I was not cut out to work in the cut-throat business world. It was not who I was. Working in this environment turned me into a very different person. For instance, I have always been, by nature, a person who takes everyone at face value. This does not serve you well in business. Relationships in the corporate world are based on maximising profit, too often by conscious manipulation - always trying to outwit the other. Eventually, I became adept at using business rules to guide my relationships. I saw financial success follow. I did not see at what cost to the people who brought me thus far in my life and who were helping me rise to this success.

As time went by, my personal relationships had become transactional and superfluous. Kind of if "If I do this for you, what will you do in return for me?" Just as in business, relationships based on vested interest always lead to gains for some and losses for others. Where had love, compassion, empathy and my passion to serve gone? This is what others, who deeply cared for me, had given to help me reach my success. I had forgotten to help my wife and children with their dreams and expectations. My business came first and they second. Money bought every comfort we could wish for, and happiness translated into how luxury could be bought. Perhaps my wife and others tagged along because they felt they had no choice, or – and I am clutching at straws - they could see what lay below my façade, hoping that one day I might come to my senses. I did not notice this loyalty, because I was not looking in their direction.

I began to develop a deep-seated fear of losing all the accumulated material comforts if something happened to the business.

I learnt that success can be a burden if it does not arise out of your natural talents and aspirations. It feels fragile, because you are not convinced that it is based upon solid foundations. Some day you have to start being the person you really are. How will the business survive when you give up the false interest in corporate strategy? What will your clients do when you prioritise your family and your true vocation? One day, the fear of being judged a failure in business will be overshadowed by the pain of separation and suffering from the love that nurtured you as a child, through university and into independent living.

Page 7

Until then, inept indecision and hollow indifference will have to do. Not being who you are, with those who know you better, distorts relationships. It confuses people, reduces their confidence in you and, ultimately, you are in danger of losing their trust. At best, you will lose the spontaneous pleasure and protective reliability of your relationships. Beyond that, loneliness and guilt await as you replay the soundtrack of what you had and did not cherish. Relationships with my brothers and their families took a new turn, too. Before we went into business together my father, two brothers and I had a beautiful relationship. We were very close and respected each other. We lived together in a big house, with plenty of land to spare.

With each addition to the family – marriages and children - we extended the house, firm in the belief that our love would hold us together. We had shared one kitchen. The children went to the same school, doctor, dentist and social functions. It was one big, happy family, with my father and mother at the head. But, alas, this was not to last long. As the business expanded, trouble started brewing. We all had specific roles delegated to us, and each of us had an agreed wage and the same benefits.

Whilst some of us were better at managing our finances, others were not. And when the better manager bought something that the others did not have, it raised awkward questions about where the money had come from.

If one, for instance, bought a bike for his child's birthday out of his own savings, the others would expect him to do the same for their children. We had simply lost faith and trust in each other. Faith and trust form the fundamental building-blocks of any kind of relationship. But both are fragile. As the saying goes, trust is hard to build and easy to break — so handle it with care. And if you fail to have faith in yourself and your decisions, it will be difficult for others to have the same regard for you.

Importantly, trust also requires transparency and clear, honest communications. This really means that we have to take responsibility for our actions, and not point fingers. And we have to be sensitive and tuned to know how the other person in the relationship feels.

And then there is the consideration of commitment to a relationship. How far are you willing to make your relationship work? And this opens up another can of worms if it is one-sided. And if it is, then we should have the skills to recognise this and have the courage to walk away.

I believe we failed in all of these aspects of building good, solid relationships. For instance, instead of lowering our expectations or backing down, in-fighting between us just got worse. There was always animosity and anger between us and, to make things worse, we lived and ate together, which made it very difficult to find a space for reflection and detox. In short, we were in each other's faces 24/7.

And that is another important point – giving or finding space in your relationships. Each individual in a relationship or commitment must have his/her own space. Space helps foster your sense of identity, individuality and autonomy, and helps you improve your commitment towards each other. Having space provides opportunities for individual growth and a sense of freedom, so that you don't feel that you are chained to the relationship partner. Perhaps the expression "familiarity breeds contempt" has merits.

We didn't create the space, and this exacerbated the situation at work and inevitable led to low work productivity. What had happened to the fun we used to have and the freedom with which we could speak about anything? Prior to these entanglements, we always lived an easy and relaxed lifestyle. Now, everyone was always on edge, speaking and treading cautiously lest the boat got rocked too much.

I know relationships between siblings can change after marriage, but this was at a different, low level.

I finally confronted my brothers about how this was affecting us. Their response was not surprising - they had their own families to look after. But should this have mattered? Wouldn't working towards a common goal improve how we looked after our families?

As I lay on the hospital bed, it dawned on me that the mostly likely reason for all these troubles was probably my fault. I was the educated one, the business had expanded when I joined them, I had seen the world and had had all the answers, I had negotiated the big contracts – long story short: "I was better than you all." And this ego just got bigger as the business got bigger.

And, finally, it gave way. This feeling of exclusivity, instead of fading away as I got more life experiences and learnt to understand different points of view and perspectives, hadn't, and resulted in an egocentric personality.

I was condescending. I didn't listen to what they were saying. I didn't appreciate the skills and experiences they brough to the job. I didn't stop to consider that they were individuals, with their own gifts and dreams. I had become judgemental and a controlling person. Not a brother or son, but a tyrant. I had become manipulative, unscrupulous and intolerant.

My non-stop pursuit of success and wealth probably meant I had set unattainable and unrealistic goals, that led to resentment and frustration. And this affected their self-esteem negatively, and any future enthusiasm for work. This is exactly what self-centred people do.

I know you may be thinking, "Hold on; this seems a bit too harsh; after all, it takes two hands to clap." But put yourselves in my shoes and imagine you are about to die. Wouldn't you want to be honest with yourselves for once and make amends before it is too late? Wouldn't you rather give the others the benefit of the doubt, and seek some sort of salvation before the lights go out?

Confronted by overwhelming emotions, to my shame I realised I was addicted to controlling others. My mind now moved to my own wife and children. How had I really treated them? Not any differently, I realised. A particular incident came to my mind.

The site manager of a major overseas construction company, in Kenya, had invited my wife and me to the club house. That was the night I was introduced to the "depth charge" - a potent combination of a shot of whisky dropped into a pint of beer. I lost count of how many I had before my wife, my 2-year-old son and I began the 120 km night journey back home. I was stark drunk.

I refused to listen to my wife, who tried desperately to stop me from driving. Halfway through the journey, I fell asleep at the wheel. I vaguely recall being shaken by the screams of my wife to wake up. As I gained some consciousness, I saw a huge warthog caught up in the headlights.

At that moment we were on Tana River Bridge, that spanned one of the largest rivers in Kenya. By some miracle, I managed to stop the car from hitting the animal and plunging, in pitch darkness, nearly 75 feet into a river. It was a fast-running, deep river that was home to hippos and crocodiles. My wife was sobbing uncontrollably, while my young son cried. I was too drunk to feel anything.

I thought it was funny at the time and, with misguided bravado, declared that being drunk sharpens your reactions to danger. What stupidity and arrogance! To this day, I still hang my head in shame whenever I recall this horrific behaviour and the imminent danger that I put my wife and child in.

I had no empathy and lived immersed in my own reality, ignoring the feelings and thoughts of others. I just wanted to look good, in a selfish and uncommitted way. I just expected every one of my relationships to act, feel and think like me. It seems I had low self-esteem, and was actually wearing a disguise to hide my deep feelings of insecurity and fear. I know I always wanted my wife to validate my opinions all the time.

I was getting deeper into my self-analysis. Believe me, I had plenty of time to reflect, in and outside the hospital. It became clear that I always sought compliments from others. I liked to be flattered, too. When you add my obsession for control to this, there is only one word to describe it – exhibitionism.

My world at this point hit rock bottom, or so I thought. My mind went back to the emotional blackmail my father had used to rope me into the business and I realised that, over time, I was doing exactly the same thing. I still had a way to go before I hit rock bottom.

My wife recalls many times where she had been driven to the precipice. It was only the belief that the old "me" she had married would surface soon that kept her from leaving. Talk of resilience! She has the patience of a saint. On the outside she never looks fazed by anything but, over the years, I have learnt to see tell-tale signs that she is near the cliff edge.

She goes very quiet – eerily quiet. I know it is time to stop pushing my luck! These days when this happens, I do not hesitate to apologise and make amends. And she just says, "It's OK." She is not - it is how hurt she feels.

My children, who are married now, have given me wonderful grandchildren. They speak about the fun they had while growing up. The trips to the water parks and game reserves, the picnics, the toys, the clothes and the beautiful places we called home.

But, sadly, when speaking of their relationship with me, they mostly remember the things I gave them, and not the love I felt for them. They tell me they were always scared of me and mostly kept out of the way. They couldn't communicate freely with me, knowing very well they would be criticised for their choices.

The memories they have of me usually begin with me saying, "I want you to… " in a tone heavily laden with the threat "or else". Now, when I see them playing with their children, I sadly wish I had been more like them. I had made myself too busy to notice, or make time for them. Who had I been working for, I often wonder?

Much to my astonishment and shock I found that I had used continued manipulation, in particular to my wife, to compensate for my insecurities. And my poor wife played along. Now I had hit rock bottom.

As I recovered, I saw the look of love and hope in the eyes of my wife and children, and knew that I had to bring a stop to my self-loathing and self-pity. I had faced my demons, the worst I was capable of being, and now had the task of rediscovering the lost soul who was full of love, compassion and laughter.

A famous poet once remarked, "Unless you tackle your demons you will never know yourself." I was reminded of a teaching in the Bible, by a Christian friend who came to visit me in hospital. Funnily enough, I had met him for the very first time at a friend's house a day before the heart attack. It is no accident that people come into your life when they do. We are all connected.

The teaching was from Mark 1:12 – "The spirit drove Jesus into the wilderness. There he would meet the wild beast. And then the angels administered to Him." The heart attack had pushed me into darkness, and I had to face the devil in me. Only then would my faith pick me up and heal me.

Psychologists rightly say that you have to have the "ego-self" to then let it go. In short, you have to have a "self" in order to go beyond the self. I had to get rid the "me" - the terrible "me" - so that the "I" could be heard. When "you" are out of the way, God can do the work. The Sikh Gurus call this state *"Vismaadh"*. You realise that God is available and accessible to pick you up.

Once I realised that I could not sink any lower, and that the only way was up, just like a mist lifting, a sense of relief, warmth and comfort washed over me. Somehow, I knew that letting go of the past was the first step to reconfiguring my life. I had to find a way to bring stability and calm to the tortured being I had become.

I wanted peace in my life, more time to be with myself and to feel more connected with all that surrounded me. I had to let go of the story that I had created about myself, and of things that didn't really matter. I had to learn to value myself again as a person. To see the light of home again.

But letting go is not easy – take my word for it; there is a crippling terror of letting go of something that has become inseparable from you. Letting go of somebody who is bad for you is the most difficult. You have to hold your breath and dive under this terror to be free of this self-imagined cage.

But, this time, I wanted to follow a different path. Musashi Miyomoto, author of the book *A Book of Five Rings: The Classic Guide to Strategy* remarks, "Even if you strive diligently on your chosen path day after day, if your heart is not in accord with it, then even if you think you are on a good path, from the point of view of the straight and true, this is not a genuine path. If you do not pursue a genuine path to its consummation, then a little bit of crookedness in the mind will later turn into a major warp. Reflect on this."

I wanted to choose a path of serving others – a path I had dreamt to walk as far back as I can remember. I was committed to not making the same, wrong choices. I was beginning to be drawn to the light of dawn. I had been offered a second chance to life, and I was not going to waste it as I had in the past. I was determined to make changes and live a life that I had dreamt about before I had allowed myself to go off track.

Louisa May Alcott, an American novelist and poet best-known as the author of the novel *Little Women* and its sequels *Little Men* and *Jo's Boys*, provides this wonderful advice: "Painful as it might be, a significant emotional event can be the catalyst for choosing a direction that serves us – and those around us – more effectively."

I saw the outpouring of love from my wife and children, and began to realise that this love had always surrounded me. I promised them that they would never be ignored or taken advantage of from this point forward. I would make sure that my work was secondary to the quality of time I spent with them. And they would have the space to flourish as individuals.

The German philosopher, Friedrich Nietzsche, had this to say; "Today as always, men fall into two groups: slaves and free men. Whoever does not have two-thirds of his day for himself, is a slave, whatever he may be: a statesman, a businessman, an official, or a scholar."

Perhaps, be more like cows. Nietzsche considered cows as the most philosophical of all the animals. They know how to sit quietly in a field, occasionally swatting away a determined fly, chewing strands of meadow grass and taking each minute as it comes.

What lent the cows their particular wisdom, in Nietzsche's eyes, was their advanced capacity not to worry overly about their own futures.

I began to see hope, as I felt myself opening the cage door and standing up again. I turned to my faith for guidance so that I could repair my broken self. I had always visited the Sikh temple but, this time around, I really wanted to 'be there as myself'.

Ken Wilber, a philosopher and mystic, in one of his Journal writings called *One Taste*, writes about how religion has performed two important functions. The first one acts as a way of creating meaning for the *separate* self. It offers myths, stories, tales, narratives, rituals and revivals that, taken together, help the separate self – the ego – to make sense of, and to endure, the slings and arrows of fortunes and the outrageous. It simply gives you a positive image – e.g. I am moral, I am a religious person and so on, and there is no change in the level of consciousness.

It consoles the self, fortifies it, defends and promotes the self. People who embrace such ideas are egocentric. The whole purpose of religion then becomes a game of reward/punishment, and not transformation. You just have to play the game right; jump a few hoops and you get your reward. This is referred to as *karma.*

The second function of religion is radical transformation. This function of religion does not fortify the separate self, but utterly shatters it. It is the transmutation and transformation of consciousness at the deepest level.

I wanted to radically transform myself. Break away from all cultural, social, religious and personal images I had built about myself. Rid myself of the past, empty my vessel and be ready to receive.

I was not going to be selfish and worry about myself all the time and never think of others. I was done trying by all means to be the centre of attention. I wanted to listen, feel, share life with others and have meaningful relationships.

I wanted to look beyond my own beliefs and opinions, and not insist that my perspectives were the right ones. I now knew these were a major source of conflict in my relationships. I wanted to adopt new ideas and have meaningful interactions in my relationships, no longer hiding behind a false facade and my weaknesses and blaming others for my shortcomings. I wanted to take criticism and use it to become better. Never feeling superior and looking down on others. I wanted my false identity to disappear, once and for all.

I was done living my life to either meet the expectations of others and blend into society or, in the other extreme, trying to impress, control and dominate. At least I did not have the added pressures of social media then. Otherwise, I would have been really busy reporting every moment of my life and desperately seeking the approval of others – likes, shares…

I was reminded of the words of Fritz Perls, in *Gestalt Therapy Verbatim*: "I do my thing and you do your thing. I am not in this world to live up to your expectations, and you are not in this world to live up to mine. You are you, and I am I, and if by chance we find each other, it's beautiful. If not, it can't be helped."

I had to find the light home and fight to get there at any cost. Find a way through the thick fog of toxic relationships I had built. The most toxic of these was the relationship – the story – the narrative – the habits and the routines – the persona I had built and believed about myself.

Alice Koller, author of the book *An Unknown Woman (1982)*, exploring the philosophical and psychological issues of self-identity, expressed the following: "I've arrived at this outermost edge of my life by my own actions. Where I am, is thoroughly unacceptable. Therefore, I must stop doing what I've been doing. This had to be my very first step towards recovery."

The truth of the matter was that change had to begin with me. The Roman orator, Marcus Tullius Cicero, remarks, "Any man can make mistakes, but only an idiot persists in his error."

On my hospital bed I prayed, and asked for guidance from the Gurus of the faith I was born into. I realised that I had to start having a different conversation with myself. I had to feel and find what was real and, for this to happen, I needed to find the space for it. I needed to know "me". I needed to listen to my inner-self and value myself as we all should.

The most time we spend is with ourselves; even when we are surrounded by people, we are still with ourselves. What must it be like not to know who we are with? Any relationship begins and ends with how well we intimately understand ourselves.

What are your likes and dislikes? What do you want from others and what can you give them? You need this understanding and personal mastery of yourself to be able to commit yourself to a relationship in the proper way, otherwise your relationships, including the one with yourself, will be superficial at best.

While I acknowledge that every relationship is "me and it" – subject-object, I was troubled by questions about how I could live freely and not be bound by it. Eli Jackson-Bear, a spiritual speaker, explains that there are different sides to this.

One side he calls the skilful means – how do we get by in the world, how do we cultivate wisdom and how do we have healthy relationships? These are skilful means and essential for quality of life. The other side is how the relationship itself becomes the doorway to the mirror, or the initiation where we must face ourselves – face the worst aspects of ourselves, what's wrong, what is bad, what we reject - and use these to release us from deeply ingrained patterns of suffering.

We have different views of the world, and the real questions are: what is this relationship, what are you expecting to get out of it, why are you in it in the first place, what is it supposed to do for you, what if it is gone, and what is it you really want?

My journey into the unknown had begun but, this time, uncertainty would be met with a warm embrace, open hands, love and excitement. Not a single step would be taken in the direction of my previous life. I looked forward to meeting "myself" after a long time.

I wanted each step to count, not only for me, but also for the people who loved me, had stuck with me and forgiven me. Dan Dennet, an American cognitive scientist and philosopher, simply says, "Find something more important than you are and dedicate your life to it."

We have to take the first step of honestly facing ourselves. We have to know who we really are at our core before we can embark on having loving and meaningful relationships. Only then can we finally let go of who we have become.

Slowly, bit by bit, the fog of falsehood will begin to lift as each layer of your self-cultivated persona is stripped away. Eventually, you will be free of the pressures that came with maintaining and sustaining these different layers. You will be free again – reborn to rediscover the gifts you were born with. In my case, my faith helped me in letting go, but it was a slow and laborious process. I was determined, however, to turn back the clock to happier times.

The comprehension that one can die without a moment's notice brings the stark realisation that a great part of our lives lies in the hands of the unknown. Our minds, however impressive, cannot peer into the future and wrest it of every last ambiguity. There are too many mind-boggling variables to consider, and peering into the future with certainty was impossible. We can't ever tell exactly what will happen to us, and nor should we try.

Letting go and accepting the idea that we cannot control our own lives, let alone those of others, is freedom from self-inflicted and self-imposed constraints on our lives. You will not be wrong in feeling uncertain and unsure of the future.

I began to see how my life over the last two decades had pushed me into a dark corner. I had got lost in a world that was alien and confusing. In the process, my living had become underpinned by self-obsession and conceit. A world full of material wealth and surrounded by people who, impressed by my achievements, called me "big boss", for the simple reason that they had their own expectations. A life of contrived parties and merry-making. A life staying busy to promote feeling "important". A life of privilege and "higher" social ranking. A life of fragile and meaningless relationships. A life away from the home, where my soul resides.

It does not take long, or a lot of effort, to fall down into the abyss of sorrow, but it does take lots of effort and time to climb back to a place of happiness and hope. The first step is to honestly face up to the worst aspects of you and take responsibility for them. As you let go of the past, you begin to get some clarity of where you want to go. You can now aim somewhere.

Are you ready to change your story and let go of relationships that no longer serve you? Take it from me, letting go is not as hard as it may seem. Look around you, and have the humility and courage to reconnect with the love, largely ignored and taken for granted, that always surrounds you. Embrace it, simply because it is the safest place to be.

Become steadfast in your quest to find meaning in your suffering, and be careful not to get caught up in self-pity and feelings of hopelessness and worthlessness. Have the courage to fix yourself, be the internal critic, repair your body and mind, be kind to yourself and begin reconnecting with your inner being.

We all have the spark of divinity within us, and should reconnect with it.

That is Chapter 2.

Chapter 2

Seeking Forgiveness and Reconciliation

It is important that we deconstruct how we live, so that we do not again get waylaid and lost. It is very easy to lose our way. We easily get distracted, give way to temptations, such as what the neighbours have that we must have. All rationalized as reasonable, of course.

As I began to deconstruct the way I had lived my working life before the heart attack, it seemed that, on both the conscious and unconscious level, I had instinctively known that I was walking on the wrong path of life and, as such, was sabotaging and resisting any form of happiness. Why, when we realise that we are following a questionable path or negotiating relationships in life that we know is not right for us, do so few of us have the courage to make changes for the better?

There may be justifiable reasons for staying on an unsatisfactory path, such as financial commitments, or waiting for a better opportunity. The problem, however, is that this gets comfortable, too, and we convince ourselves that this is what we prefer to the now 'distant' needs and aspirations we were once in contact with.

This is basically an addiction, which is to pursue a behaviour compulsively in spite of negative consequences.

As in any addiction, that first step to recovery is acknowledging the addiction. I had to make a concerted effort to change the way I thought and made decisions. I didn't want to keep on making excuses to maintain the conditions that had eventually resulted in a heart attack. I have to admit that I felt an overwhelming sense of panic at the thought of breaking away from what was so familiar and easy to fall back onto.

It is the same feeling you get when you think about giving up a personal relationship. You feel great anxiety and fear, that make you want to cling to it even more. When you try to take steps to end it, you suffer withdrawal systems that can include both emotional and physical stress. The only way you feel relieved is when you re-establish contact with the person.

By carefully breaking down the reasons behind my current situation, I was able to get a better understanding of a way forward. I had already acknowledged my shortcomings, and had felt that my understanding of what was really important to me was still intact. Now I wanted to reconnect with what was of deeper value in my life, and allow the sunshine back in.

I took some guidance from the author, Robin Norwood, who says that "The first was to make recovery a priority and making sure that you had all the support that you required to succeed. You also had to develop a spiritual side and engage in daily activities that increased your own sense of peace and tranquillity."

We have to be careful how we move forward. Too often, we look for solutions before fully understanding and accepting the facts of the current situation. It is important to pay close attention to real issues, their causes and impacts, so that we do not slip back into the addictive state. We are clever at restating issues and concerns so that the answer is to not change significantly, or that others must change.

Memories and feelings of a life that was happy and carefree provides me with a different way to live. It strengthens hope and optimism of how life can be, because you have actually experienced it. I reminisced about my childhood a lot after the heart attack. It was a place that felt like a safe haven, a sanctuary where I felt safe and comfortable with myself. A place where I had always been embraced by love. A place that I could momentarily visit when the current reality of what I had now become could be forgotten.

Life was simple then, and it did not take a lot to make us happy when we were young. We were mostly content, apart from the occasional punishment we received when we were overly mischievous. We also invented and made our own toys from discarded items and whatever we could use from nature – bushes and trees, or discarded rubbish – plastic bottles, metal bottle-tops, string and so on.

I remember fondly a favourite game my brother and I used to play in the veranda of our flat. Pretending to be engineers from the local electricity company, we used to climb the corner pole in the veranda using our father's trouser-belt as the safety harness. We stuck some forks and spoons into our shorts for tools. The only drawback was that we only had access to my dad's belt when he used to be off work. Sadly, my brother and I haven't spoken for years. We just forgot to be ourselves, and who we were in simpler times.

Pretending is fun when we were small boys, but a source of pain in adult life. We are naturally happy in our uncomplicated pretend game but, as we get older, in the "real" world, it often appears that we prefer to be worried and sad rather than be happy. A part of you is still a child. It is important to keep this. It lets you feel your own history and gives you a sense of stability through being rooted. Different experiences in our childhood shape what we want in our adult life. These experiences helped to meet our needs. Our needs now can be met by similar experiences of our choosing.

I recall, with fondness, the time my father took me to the city to buy me a gift of my choice. I was 18, and travelling to the USA for university. I couldn't remember ever being alone with him before that trip to the city. Just to be alone in his presence for a whole day felt really special and, to this day, that day spent with my father was the best gift anyone has ever given me.

He bought me a Timex wristwatch, and I still remember the shop, which was in the famous *Thorn Tree Hotel*. It got its name from the acacia tree around which the hotel was built. It was an exclusive shopping complex, frequented by the rich, where only the best quality items were sold.

The complex always smelled of coffee and fresh pastries, and was full with the chatter of visiting tourists. I felt proud, privileged and important to be in the complex with him. In that moment, I pledged never to let him down. Just being alone with him had made me feel important, special and privileged.

Sadly, many years later, I did let him down several times. I had become too cocky from the education that I had received in the USA, that he had paid for. It is sad that the gifts of education and general wellbeing that our parents - and others that love and care about us — give us, are taken for granted.

These gifts of love — from many relationships - are provided to us from a place of unconditional acceptance. We assume their support, no matter what happens. We expect it, and take the source for granted. It is too late to give back when they are longer with us.

Life is a precious gift that we take for granted. The British portrait painter of the 17th and 18th centuries, Sir Godfrey Kneller, remarked, "To think creatively, we must be able to look afresh at what we normally take for granted."

I remember the look of sadness on my father's face when he saw me off at the airport. I knew, in that moment, that he had always loved me, although he had never expressed it in explicit terms. And, sadly, I hadn't either.

I realised with a great sense of regret, especially now that he is no longer with us, that he was a loving man, and he went from this world not really knowing or feeling love. He had worked very hard all his life to make me who I am today. I had not appreciated or acknowledged the important and vital role he had played in my life. I had taken him for granted. This felt painful, and still does.

I reminded myself of how we experienced love and affection from other communities whilst growing up. There was one particular example that I always share with my grandchildren whenever I can get them to put the iPads down.

Only a few households had television sets in the 70s, and programmes usually started at 4.30 in the afternoon and lasted until midnight. And there was only one channel. There was a Gujarati family living down the road who would on some occasions allow us to watch cartoons – Popeye the Sailor, Hercules, Felix the Cat – for 20 minutes or so.

They would sit on their sofas while my brothers and sisters sat on the floor. We didn't judge them and were grateful for their kindness. Once the programme had finished, each of us would thank the host and leave quietly, hoping they would allow us back another time. If we were lucky, we would get to watch 3 or 4 episodes in a month.

The sense of community was strong, and it seemed that shortcomings in one's personal circumstances were met by others without awkward questions or being looked down upon. These relationships were built on the gifts of love, respect and compassion.

There were no demands or expectations – you just knew intuitively that you were surrounded by support when needed. It was pure simplicity. These days, it's very difficult to feel this community spirit and distinguish between fake and real relationships. The world has become very competitive, and the prescription for success seems to be being independent and aggressive. Loneliness has become a chronic disease in today's society.

We are too casual and liberal on how we use words – perhaps not realising the scaredness and the depth of meaning they express.

But, sadly, I had followed a path that was full of cracks and breakages. In the process, I had hurt a lot of people. I knew I had to seek forgiveness and reconciliation from all those I had hurt and let down. Then I could learn to forgive myself, too. Lewis B. Smedes, a renowned Christian author, writes, "To forgive is to set a prisoner free and discover that the prisoner was you."

It became clearer to me as time went by that, whilst seeking forgiveness was important, it had a tinge of selfishness. Given my past history, why would anybody trust that I meant what I said? That is why the process of reconciliation was also as important as forgiveness.

Reconciliation involves communication between two people, and this can lead to really experiencing forgiveness. My efforts at this provided me with an opportunity to explain, to those I had hurt, that I really understood and regretted how I had behaved. When I spoke, it also brought out other emotions - shame, conceit, etc. – which were bubbling under the surface.

Page 29

Reconciliation is about restoring trust and, unlike forgiveness, requires the active participation and cooperation of the other person. I knew my sincere regrets could only be expressed fully if, through mutual dialogue, they brought a sense of justice to those whom I had hurt.

I can say confidently that, without forgiveness, reconciliation is not possible. And that forgiveness on its own is never enough if you are really earnest in repairing your relationships.

Furthermore, take it from me that both forgiveness and reconciliation are also fundamentally important within yourself. It's a win-win situation, but it takes courage and humility. Severity, denial, or grovelling when seeking forgiveness and reconciliation, are counterproductive. As Martin Luther King Jr, the activist, so eloquently puts it, "Darkness cannot drive out darkness; only light can do that. Hate cannot drive out hate; only love can do that."

I found that how I communicated played an important role in how effective forgiveness and the reconciliation process were. Empirical research carried out by Waldron and Kelly, in 2005, found that "Conditional communication was linked to relationship deterioration after the episode of forgiveness, but more genuine and explicit strategies that included nonverbal expressions of forgiveness contributed to relationship strengthening."

My father had a plaque at home that simply read, "Charity begins at home." It is sad that we remember wise words only when things go wrong or, worse still, when the ones who said them are gone. Simple words that said to me, "Put your own house in order first." These are the relationships that we appreciate the least.

We have relationships that are so deep and meaningful that we just do not appreciate their value, or the important role they play in shaping our lives. These relationships include everyday interactions that, on the surface, don't look important but, deep down, are forming who we are or become, including the way we perceive and act in the world.

I sought forgiveness from my father as soon as I was able to. He sounded tired and defeated. I had not fulfilled his dreams. But he was a forgiving man and simply said, "What happened has happened – let us be more careful in the future." I should have been truthful with him. Be truthful, with sensitivity. Say it not with acceptance out of fear, nor to reject and demean another person or their ideas. Say it to bring clarity about what seems best for both of you. The other person's reaction may not be in your control. Whatever it is, face it. You are not here to allow misunderstandings and subsequent resentment out of fear of saying what you feel or want. You are here to play a part in helping all our lives improve. Doing what you know you will not commit to, or not want to learn about, will make you live with your heart and soul suppressed. No one can live like that.

I had certainly taken them for granted, and hadn't expressed my gratitude for all the sacrifices he had made for my siblings and, more especially, me. There were many times that we I had spoken to him in a manner that had tones of anger and hate.

In all relationships, we want to be appreciated. Little acts of appreciation can make a big difference to our relationships. Simply acknowledging, and being thankful for, all these gifts re-connects us to each other. But we get used to everyday things being done for us and, sadly, never show appreciation for them. Expressing appreciation to those who bring us everyday gifts is important. A lesson learnt late in life.

I thought about how hurt my mother must have been. She must have suffered terribly, seeing me change so much. She also had great expectations of me and hoped I could look after her in her old age. I had let her down, too. But she had a compassionate and forgiving heart, and simply said get better, recover and start again. Everybody makes mistakes - just don't make them again. Look after your family. Honoré de Balzac, the French novelist, writes, "The heart of a mother is a deep abyss, at the bottom of which you will always find forgiveness."

I sought forgiveness and reconciliation from my siblings. We all made an effort, but it seemed we had drifted too far apart. Recently, my mother passed away and I made another effort. As the prayers for her departure from this life were concluded at the temple, I stood up in the congregation, the sangat, and asked for forgiveness. I pleaded that both our parents had gone and that they went away in pain, knowing their own children were not speaking to each other.

I felt at peace that I had made several efforts, and now time would tell what would happen to these relationships. I have hope, because I did what my Guru had advised me. In one of his teachings he says, "Where there is forgiveness there is the Guru himself." I have faith.

My wife and kids were forgiving, and showed understanding and compassion. They had always been forgiving, even in my worst moments. I felt humbled and thankful that I was surrounded by such unconditional love. Bryant H. McGill, an American author and speaker, says, "There is no love without forgiveness and there is no forgiveness without love." That is all I needed to know.

My wife had always been committed to me, and I know for a fact that the willingness to forgive is related to the level of commitment and trust. I work hard to regain this trust. I know forgiveness is not always easy and it feels painful. I know I had wounded her, but we both know that there is no peace without forgiveness.

I worked hard to continually show her how valued and important she is to me. I started by opening up to her about my emotions. We communicate much more openly and freely now. This is the key to our strong relationship. I truly believe that seeking forgiveness is a spiritual discipline. As on a spiritual journey, forgiveness begins by first recognising where we are at a certain point in time, and what can be done to improve it. It is accompanied by emotions such as regret or despair, which act as triggers for change.

I also learnt that, with some of the relationships I was repairing, it requires just a matter of clearing the air. If this were done on a more conscious level, I could avoid the cumulative effects of smaller things becoming huge.

Now that I had begun do get some clarity and perspective to my life, it was important to move beyond the suffering. Now it was crucial to understand it, and form a clear and precise picture of it.

That is Chapter 3.

Chapter 3

Finding Meaning In My Suffering

It didn't take long for the reality of my extreme health condition to sink in. When it did, and the realisation dawned that death was literally a heartbeat away, the world that I had known exploded and vaporised.

My grief was acute, and I was plagued by nightmares, anxiety and depression which persisted for a long time. I looked around the hospital room. There were other patients recovering from heart attacks. I was the youngest. We were all waiting for an angiogram.

The oldest must have been over 75, and his bed was nearest to the door. He had been in hospital for some time and was always speaking about his son. In the few days that he was in the ward, he never got a visit from him. He passed away one early morning, and that was my first experience of a body bag.

This experience hit me like a bolt of lightning. I could have been in that body bag; I could still be next. It was a moment of stark realisation that I wasn't invincible after all. What really struck me was that nobody had cared enough for this man to visit him. What had he done in life not to be surrounded by family or friends? Another patient was in his 50s. He told me this was his second heart attack, in a tone that sounded as if it were just normal. I don't mean this to sound like he didn't care or worry. He was just resigned to the fact that he had a problem, that life was fragile and, instead of worrying about events that he had no control over, he just got on with it.

He didn't have any visitors, either, because he had not told anybody he was in hospital. He said he didn't want anybody to worry, and that he would just catch the bus home. I wondered what led to this attitude. The Jewish-Dutch philosopher, Spinoza, says in his *Ethics*, "Affectus, qui passioest, desinit esse passio simulatque eius claram et distinctam formamus ideam" which means "Emotion, which is suffering, ceases to be suffering as soon as we form a clear and precise picture of it."

Page 35

The look of desperation and impending loss on the faces of my wife and children were a constant reminder of why I had to not simply survive, but also to change and turn our lives around. I had put them through enough pain already, and it was time for me to help bring happiness back into our lives. I now had a reason - the "why" – for motivation. I am reminded of how Frankl uses Nietzsche's words, "He who has a *why* to live for can bear with almost any *how*," to give meaning to the terrible things that happened in a Nazi concentration camp.

As I coped with these struggles and witnessed, first-hand, others struggling like me in the same room, I began to look at ways my own devastation could become more bearable. Slowly, bit by bit, I began a process of making meaning out of my misery. The psychiatrist and Holocaust survivor, Viktor Frankl, wrote extensively about this process after observing that his fellow inmates in concentration camps were more likely to survive the horrific conditions if they held on to a sense of meaning and purpose.

Jordon Peterson, author and psychologist, encourages people who are struggling, and have more or less given up, to pick up the courage and take aim, any aim. Its trajectory can always be adjusted as we get better at what we are doing.

I knew that my motivation for change had to come from life changes. I had to find a way to fix myself by embracing my new health situation, as if it were a dear, close, delicate flower.

I had heard about the power of prayer and that, with faith and believing, miracles happened. I had also read somewhere about how the power of the brain helped the healing process. Our bodies have the power to heal and repair themselves. I truly believe this because a few years after the heart attack, and with other changes in my life, including completely changing my mental framework, I work and live like a person who has a normal heart.

It's been over twenty years and, with a changed attitude, I went back to university at the age of 40 and, within 5 years, had graduated with a Master's degree in Science, and a Doctorate – PhD. I worked at the university and, later, for an NGO in the Netherlands, and started my own not-for-profit organisation, working on projects all over the world. In that time, I experienced the most wonderful relationships with my wife, children, friends and colleagues.

I now had a greater appreciation of life. You would, too, if you experienced at first-hand the fragility of life. In a wink, without notice, you could be snuffed out. You wouldn't even know that you had died! Gone also would be all your ego, self-worth, dreams, ambitions, plans, relationships, Ferrari and whatever you think defines you.

I now looked at life and its offerings with gratitude and renewed optimism. The Sikh Gurus call this *"chardi kala"* – always in grace and acceptance, no matter the challenge. Take it from me, you really begin to appreciate your five senses then. Every taste, touch, sight, note, or smell reinvigorates you. Imagine what it does to your relationships. How would you treat somebody if you knew this was the last time you would ever speak to, touch, hear or see them? Would there be any space for old grudges, criticisms, judgements, or expectations?

Page 37

The Japanese have a wonderful tradition. When guests leave their house, they will stand outside their house and wave at the guests driving off, until they are out of sight. The reason – this might be the last time they see their guests. Powerful and moving stuff.

I have made reference several times before to the powerful role that spirituality can play in your life. Not only in finding meaning in your suffering but much beyond, in how your life can become more meaningful. For me, it was not about asking questions about the existence of God.

I had been brought up in a Sikh family. With shame, I admitted to myself that I had succumbed to what Richard Dawson, in his book *God Delusion*, called "lazy temptation."

Following my faith reduced to rituals and weekly visits to the temple, mainly to enjoy an evening out with friends. Rarely practising the teachings of the Gurus that guided us to be compassionate, forgiving, without judgements, love and justice. But I believe with all my heart that we are not alone. There is nothing to be afraid of. I hung on to this as I prayed for forgiveness and guidance. My faith provided me with the courage and certainty that there was meaning in my suffering. Everything happened according to His will. I had survived because He wanted to show me a different path in life, as a shepherd does to his lost sheep.

The most powerful motivators for seeking meaning in my suffering were relationships. It is true that suffering brings people closer, beginning with the immediate family that kept vigil at my bedside. Then there were the strangers who were looking after me. And there are those who are going through suffering, just like yourself. And let us not forget our friends and well-wishers, without judging their sincerity. And what about those who provide spiritual support? The Sikh Gurus call this community with a common purpose of keeping each other well, the *sadh sangat*.

Also called the *congregation, the sangha, the minyan* and the *halka*. If we give ourselves a moment to reflect on the relationships we now have, you will be surprised to note that you are already surrounded by such gifts. The problem has been that we have been looking through the lens of ego. What am I receiving? How much is it putting me at the top of the pile? Rather than, why do I deserve this? How can I give something back to others?

All that is needed is an acknowledgement that we are always surrounded by love, and then these gifts are seen in all shapes and forms. These might just be a glimmer of a smile on the face of another, an act of kindness from a stranger, an embrace from a loved one, the freshness of the air we breathe, the taste of the food we eat, or simply being in the safe and comfortable presence of someone. By recognising that I was already surrounded by love, I learnt to be grateful for what I already had.

As I recovered I knew that, without the courage to rise and compassion to give, I could not have relationships that would bring out the best in me. I certainly don't want to go back to my earlier days. Without relationships, I cannot know myself and, without knowing myself, I could not find meaning in my life.

Page 39

Someone once said, "Love is giving someone the ability to destroy you, but trusting them not to. Without a doubt, when it comes to matters of the heart in regards to love, you can most definitely allow yourself to experience absolute vulnerability knowing full well that particular person has the power to destroy you physically, mentally, emotionally, and spiritually as well.

"Destroy you in such a way the inner turmoil you go through leaves you with a tightened sensation within your chest so that it's hard for you to even breathe. Yet, even though you may have this overwhelming sense of fear concerning getting hurt by a certain special someone, you inevitably put all your trust in him/her, leaving you with this sense of peaceful calm you can't explain; to the point where, during the times you continue to spend with him/her, you begin to breathe easier and easier."

Well, I experienced this first-hand. Here is what happened.

I fell madly in love at 17 (as far as you are able to at age 17). I saw her for the first time at the temple, and it just happened – struck by a bolt of lightning. There was no time to reflect about how I felt. It felt so natural and right. Until then, love was just a word, but she gave it meaning.

But she needed some convincing. I tried every trick in the book to get her attention – humour, dressing-up smart and gifts (mostly from my lunch money), but she didn't show much interest. I could only think of her and nothing else.

On occasion she would show some sign of acknowledgement of my existence, but this was rare. But I kept up the chase, hoping to eventually wear her down. Perhaps she showed the occasional interest to keep me at bay. Perhaps she felt scared of her parents, or perhaps she was beginning to melt. I could only hope.

And, on the rare occasion she smiled at me, or accepted a gift, I felt like the luckiest person alive. I bathed in the warmth of joy. I declared my feelings on every opportunity, but she never reciprocated. She kept me wondering. But she was very polite and, in her husky voice, spoke with respect. She drew me in even closer. But she never declared her love for me, nor did she reject me. She kept me hanging and hoping.

But then, one day, I picked up the courage to go to her house to say goodbye. I was leaving the country to study in India. I got to the top of the three flights of stairs, praying that she be alone. I knocked on the sliding grill, ready with my excuses if it was opened by her mother or father.

She was all alone, and my happiness knew no bounds. I had never been so scared and nervous but, as soon as my eyes saw her, nothing else mattered. She was shocked to see me and, for a moment, I braced myself for the worst, but her eyes said something else and she invited me in.

I noticed a piece of paper and pen on the dining table that she quickly tried to hide. She finally showed me the paper. She had been writing to me. It began, "Dearest Tari (my nickname), you must have been too busy to come to see me. Anyway, the things that we wish sometimes cannot come true."

In that one instant, everything came to a standstill — it was as if I were born for this moment — the peak of my existence. We spoke for the first time about our feelings, and she told me how she feared we would never be together. We were from different castes, and her father would never allow it. And that is why she had held back.

Page 41

She knew I was going away to study, and felt that she had to write to me and share her feelings and fears. Later, I took the unfinished letter and set of cuff links she had bought for me as a memento. Little did I know that these would be the last words we would share as, a year later, she married someone else.

I was heartbroken, and I turned to the unfinished letter and the cuff links umpteen times for comfort. Much later, I saw her again. We were on different paths, but…

Yet, I am ever-grateful for this painful experience. She had showed me what touching love felt like. Love through conscious presence, one in essence, so natural, peaceful, so fulfilling. Love without doing anything, without cultivation. Such a wonderful and invaluable gift.

My wife showed me what true love and commitment meant. No matter what, she stuck with me, and I fell in love more deeply and with more of my being. That love is the only constant that there is - all other love is a version of this. Importantly, my wife showed me that love is never selfish – it is self-less. Martin Luther King, quoting Shakespeare, said, "Love is a steadfast." Now, that is a man who knew a thing or two about love.

She showed me that true love is a conscious presence, when you recognise that there is a place greater than the person. It feels so natural, so effortless, so simple, so total, so content, so happy, so loving, and yet you realise you are not doing anything to be like this. I am not doing love, I am not doing peace, it's just like it's here, between us, and we don't know where it has come from.

This love is not cultivated – it's just there – it just happens. Yes, you can learn to love one another, God, yourself, but this is not learnt. It just pours out of you and you don't even have to keep it up, keep it going with effort - it's just there, like the perfume and the flower.

True love is not something you do – give and take – it's just the basis or foundation of all that exists – and within this love there is room for the play of hate or resistance, simply because it is greater than them.

I saw my first love many years after my marriage, and discovered that her first real love had always been someone else. For a while I was devastated that it had not been me, but then recalled the feeling of love that the words of her unfinished letter brought in me. I was grateful to be graced with that love, if only for a moment.

We sometimes receive gifts that bring us pain and misery. They made you who you are today. Now those experiences – gifts – might have made you a very bitter and sad person but, if you can reflect on this and face these experiences head-on, you can find the courage and compassion to forgive those who hurt you.

Jill Bolte Taylor, a Harvard-trained brain scientist, experienced a complete shutdown of the left hemisphere (which is responsible for linear, logical and critical thinking) of her brain as a result of a massive stroke, caused by a ruptured blood vessel. She teaches that we each have the power to purposefully choose to "step to the right of our left hemispheres" and connect with the incredible peace and joy that she experienced.

Gibran Khalil, an American academic, shares these wise words of wisdom; "I have learnt silence from the talkative, tolerance from the intolerant, kindness from the unkind yet I am ungrateful to them."

I had finally found meaning in my suffering. I could see new possibilities and opportunities ahead. I could envision the bright, joyous future that I had always wanted. I was not ashamed and depressed about my past. I could plan with the belief that I was not alone. I had always been surrounded by offerings and gifts, but had not seen them. Now I could. I had purpose.

Victor Frankl, during his time in the concentration camp, found that those around him who did not lose their sense of purpose and meaning in life were able to survive much longer than those who had lost their way. I think this is, perhaps, what Frankl meant when he said that, "It is life itself that asks questions of man." He further adds that, "It is not enough simply to have something to do, rather what counts is the manner in which one does the work."

My life was going to be fresh, exciting and full of love, laughter and joy. Not in pursuit of happiness, or some other Utopian view of life but to – pardon the expression – let the chips fall where they may and yet still make meaning of life. Not to be in despair or suffering, but to look for meaning from whatever presents itself in the moment. Not to pursue happiness, but to let it ensue. And that, as I found out, was a profound discovery that guides me in everyday living. Giving love, happiness, relationships and "things" room to breathe and come to you.

These reflections, on offerings and gifts in my life in happier times, provided new direction, motivation and courage to face myself head-on and look beyond the pretentious, personal image I had cultivated for over 20 years. Osho, an Eastern mystic, once remarked, "I am going to live the way I want to live. I am going to live in my own spontaneity and authenticity. I am not here to fulfil anybody's expectations."

I wanted to live once again on my own terms, and fulfil dreams that I once had before I allowed myself to get caught in a life that felt alien. To be spontaneous and free of expectations of society. To live fearlessly and in freedom. These were the gifts I wanted in my life. I acknowledged that change was a part of life, and that it had to be accepted with grace. Change brought with it new challenges, and a renewal of life itself.

I am reminded of Makoto Shinkai's film, *5 Centimetres Per Second*, in which he subverts typical romantic norms in favour of a more realistic portrayal of love and relationships. 5 centimetres per second is the rate at which a cherry blossom falls to the ground. By the time it has hit the ground, it has changed. Natural things change, and so do you. Yes, we all change; I had to, but how, and why?

I always watch with interest my grandchildren playing with *Lego*. They construct amazing things- fitting the same pieces in a number of different ways. They have a general idea of what they want to create, but have no specific image of the final result.

They are spontaneous, excited and happy, whatever the outcome.

I realised that is exactly what my life is like now. Different *Lego* pieces are thrown at me every day and I choose, in the moment, how to make meaning of life. There are no expectations of a specific result, and it is always fun, because I can decide what to create and how to do so.

Before the heart attack, in pursuit of a perfect future life, I had no time for myself. I did not know this then, but realise now that, even when I was with my family on a free day, my mind was always elsewhere. I was always planning the next move. It had become a habit. I remember feeling a sense of guilt on public holidays, when work had to stop.

I was with my family, but the feeling that I should be elsewhere, or doing something work-related, never left me. What did this say about the value I placed upon my nearest and dearest?

Compare this to this morning. It is 17th July 2018 and my close friend, Mehar, and I were having a cup of tea and the usual accompaniments. This always puts me in a great place. It is not just the company and the tea, but the free, uninhibited flow of conversation between two friends. No pretentions or expectations.

We were discussing this book and going through what I had written so far; I was rather pleased with my fifth attempt and expecting great feedback. I could see him struggling after the first paragraph. He is a teacher and school inspector, you see. After careful thought, he spoke with a voice that was kind, yet assertive.

"What are you trying to say here?" he asked. As I re-read the paragraph, I mumbled, with the realisation that the paragraph conveyed no personal story and read like an academic research paper.

The choice of words says something about our personalities, as they are an expression of our thoughts and feelings. We can tell from words whether someone is being honest, or consciously manipulative.

I was suddenly awash with a feeling of warmth and respect for him. His words were simple and conveyed sincerity. He had, time and again, demonstrated compassion and love, even when least expected, for my family and myself.

There is an unspoken, unfettered bond between us. He was being "him", and I "me". No camouflage. Each is not trying to out-think the other, or have a battle of wits. It's just honest talk, right from the heart. We can share our inner thoughts without feeling weak, vulnerable, out of control, or less powerful.

What a wonderful, valuable gift of friendship we share. We both value the chance of speaking freely, showing kindness, and helping each other understand more and become a little more of what we want to be.

Relationships are one of the most effective ways of flourishing in life, because you are "really there" for each other.

That is Chapter 4.

Chapter 4

Rewriting My Own Story

Sick and tired of abusing and abandoning myself, I wanted to be fully present so that I could find peace and happiness in my life. I wanted the opportunity to live on my own terms and not seek validation from others.

Dale Carnegie, an American writer and lecturer, writes, "It is the way we react to circumstances that determines our feelings," or "It isn't what you have, or who you are, or where you are, or what you are doing that makes you happy or unhappy. It is what you think about."

I wanted to follow my heart's desires. "Not because it's the perfect time to make ourselves better," writes Sara Witzler, in her blog *How Changing the Story in My Head Changed My Life*, "but because we have already been amazingly shiny and beautiful without even realizing it. It's time to peel away the layers, pull back the veils, remove the tarnish we have covered ourselves in for years. Decades. Lifetimes."

And she continues, "When I came to yoga, I was a shattered human being. After years of practice and peeling off the layers (upon layers, upon layers) I began to recover my wholeness. After all of that work and all of that time, my life has changed... but the highlight reel, the story in my head has not. In my old story, I am not good enough." I was desperate to strip myself of an image of myself I had created over the last 25 years. A persona that I myself was ashamed of and disgusted with. It was time to face myself with honesty, and brutal honesty.

I had developed deep wounds over the years through repeated behaviours that made me unhappy and hurt those around me.

I had to find a way to go beyond these pains and get to a place that was the core of myself; to the heart of my spirit, where I could find the light and warmth of my own core qualities of love and peace. My Sikh faith had always made it abundantly clear that we are the spirit which is eternally present within us. That spirit protects and loves at all levels, and is all that we need to heal our inner wounds.

I had to begin a journey of finding out who the real me was. Charles Bukowski, a German-born American poet and novelist, remarked, "Can you remember who you were, before the world told you who you should be?"

I remember, right from a very young age, whenever anybody used to ask me what I wanted to do or become when I became an adult. I would always say I wanted to be able to walk down a street and have people say, "That person really helped me." Right from a very young age, I had always wanted to serve others. I had been so sure of what I wanted to be and do.

Flourishing Relationships

"What do you do for a living?" was the question that most people asked when I was released from hospital. A bizarre question to ask somebody who has just come home after a near-death experience, I thought. I suppose people identify with the role one plays, rather how a person feels. My youngest daughter, Aman, has a mind of her own. She is one person who clearly, from a very young age, understood who she was and wanted in life. She was focused, and aimed for that one thing that made her tick. She wanted to work in the film industry as a camera engineer, travel and see the world.

So, she went to university and, later, to a well-known film studio, to learn about the practical aspects of film-making. Many a time, whilst working on film sets as an unpaid camera trainee, she was treated like a nobody.

It really upset her, but she kept at it, never giving up on her dreams. Never selling herself short or letting herself down. She knew what she wanted and the skills she needed to succeed, and she kept at it. Later she wrote, directed and produced a couple of short films, and got an award for one of them.

And then she got her dream job. The first female movie-camera engineer with a well-known, world-class, movie equipment provider. She now goes to work every day without complaining, travels the world expenses paid, and is always chirpy. She has a fantastic relationship with her work colleagues, friends and family. Only because she knew who she was and stuck to what she wanted, right from a very young age. She was in her element.

Finding your element is to know yourself. To begin with, it means that you are doing something for which you have a natural feel. If you can catch a glimmer of your gift, or your natural element, then you will really understand what it means to be truly free. Being in your element is more than knowing what you are good at. To be in your element is to really love what you do. Confucius said, "Choose a job you love, and you will never have to work a day in your life."

In the family business, I had always been afraid of failure and, especially, of what other people would think if I did fail. I know now this is an indicator of disempowerment – always looking outside of myself to fill something that only I could have filled. Dale Carnegie, an author of several books, including *How to Win Friends and Influence People* (1936), asks some very important questions - "Did you ever see an unhappy horse? Did you ever see a bird that had the blues? One reason why birds and horses are not unhappy is because they are not trying to impress other birds and horses."

I know no amount of external approval can make me feel complete or whole. I know that, even when I was seeking approval, it could come a couple of times but not always, which, in turn, brings you into further suffering. Seeking approval is an addictive cycle that turns you away from yourself.

Please don't get me wrong. I am not recommending completely not caring about other people, or what they think about us. I am only saying we should look after ourselves, too. The thing I do suggest is that you remind yourselves of who you really are, and use this and anchor yourself in your scared space. This way you can venture out whenever and wherever you are knowing that you are the sacred self.

Completely out of my element, I had become dependent on the outcome in a game I didn't want to play in the first place. I was born with my own special gift and, in order to live it, I had to step fearlessly and confidently beyond the mundane and my comfort zone.

I am reminded what Pierre Teihard de Charding, a French idealistic philosopher and Jesuit priest, said about fear – "Instead of standing on the shore and proving to ourselves that the ocean cannot carry us, let us venture on its waters just to see."

Easier said than done, you might say. But when you have had an experience like mine, it's not too difficult to remind yourself not to wander off too far in the wrong direction. Having an aim – pointing somewhere – keeps you on the ball.

In order to change, we have to be able to see ourselves, accept who we are by giving ourselves love, then make choices that will make life more meaningful and have relationships that really matter. In my particular situation I have relationships with those who stood by me when I fumbled. They are the ones who mattered because, through them, I could see what I had become and what I could become.

Relationship itself can be the mirror where we must face ourselves – face the worst aspects of ourselves, what's wrong, what is bad and what we reject. We are all acting as mirrors for one another. We learn to discover who we are through the eyes of others, and every person we meet during the course of our lives can bring us something different. The eminent psychologist,

Carl Gustav Jung, said, "The encounter of two people is like the contact of two chemical substances: if there is any reaction, both are transformed."

Staring death staring in the face forced me to the realisation that there were no guarantees as to how long you live, and the time to act was now. I wanted to be the best version of myself. I had already faced and practised the worst I could be. "Don't try to be the broken version of someone else. Be the best version of yourself and your own biggest fan," says Michelle D'Avella, an author and mentor.

But there were still issues that I needed to sort out in my head. I needed first to accept responsibility for the actions and choices I had made. Secondly, it was imperative that I chose wisely the path I wanted to follow. For this I needed not only clarity of thought, but also the faith that I was being looked after by something bigger than all of us. I once again turned to my Sikh faith for guidance.

As I practised the teachings of my Gurus, that included meditation (jap) and community services (sewa), I became more centred. Self-reflection forced me to face, and take responsibility for, my present situation. There was nobody else to blame. I had begun the process of change and self-discovery; to leave behind an unfulfilling life and to grow and fulfil a childhood dream. The psychologist, Carl Jung, makes a remarkable observation; "We don't solve our problems," he says, "we outgrow them."

Mike Robbins, author of the book *Bring Your Whole Self to Work* says, "We've all experienced this outgrowing process many times. Think back to some of the biggest 'problems' in your life, when you were a child or an adolescent (or even just a few years or months ago), that are no longer issues for you anymore. In most cases, you simply outgrew these things." He continues, "We also experience this phenomenon whenever something intense happens in our life – whether it's something that is intensely 'good' or 'bad'. Major life experiences will often put things in perspective – giving us an opportunity to stop and re-evaluate many aspects of our lives. Often, upon further reflection, we realize that most of our 'problems' are not that big of a deal."

He suggests making this process "more conscious and deliberate, and not simply happen by accident. It's important that we shift our focus, as Jung reminds us, from 'solving' to 'growing'. As we try to 'solve' the biggest problems in our lives – related to relationships, career, health, effectiveness, money, awareness, and more – maybe we can stop trying so hard to 'fix' these things and look more deeply at the feedback we're getting and where we can enhance our growth."

He suggests we try the following three things to think about as we look to deepen our growth and shift away from the obsessive problem-solving mode many of us find ourselves in:

First, confront your biggest "problems". Tell the truth about the biggest issues in your life and look at what you've been doing to either avoid or solve them – neither of which will ultimately give you what you want.

Second, look for the growth opportunity. With authenticity and compassion, see if you can look beneath your avoidance, or even your intended solutions, and look for the beautiful feedback life is giving you right now about where you can grow.

And, thirdly, reach out for support. Getting support, feedback and guidance is an essential aspect of our life and growth, especially when we want to change, transform and grow into new and deeper places. When we're looking at outgrowing some of the most challenging aspects of our life and transcending certain problems (some of which we may have been dealing with for quite some time), it is fundamentally important we reach out for help from people in our lives – friends, family members, co-workers, counsellors, coaches, teachers and others.

As we do these three things, with a sense of kindness and appreciation towards ourselves, we can expand our growth, which will ultimately lead us to where we want to be in our lives. Remember, there is no specific "destination" we're after in this process – growth is really about deepening our experience of life and enhancing our capacity for joy, fulfilment and love. I fully agree with Mike. The Sanskrit word Udaseenta comes from two words: *Ud*, which means "above", and *assen*, meaning "to sit". To be *udaseen* means to rise above the level we are currently at. It describes a path of rising above desire. In short, a path of continuous improvement that implies internal development which leads to overcoming emotional and mental suffering. I was ready to begin rewriting my own story.

I had taken an honest look at myself, the decisions and actions that had brought me to this point. I wanted to write a story that held no grudges or resentment. The story would be framed in the positive – what the Sikh Gurus call *chardi kala* – my glass does not have to be full, but overflowing. I had seen the gifts and offerings that surrounded me all the time. I would use the lessons learnt in my old life in a new light, and pursue my natural element.

In order to rewrite this story, I would have to go beyond fear and bring courage and compassion into my everyday living. The Sikh faith provides several tools for everyday living. Guidance that provides a perspective to life that brings peace of mind, compassion, forgiveness and contentment.

That is Chapter 5.

Chapter 5

Moving Towards What Matters Most

I had to learn to accept life as it happens. To break the downward spiral of pessimism, and imagining that one event that was not I had wanted leads to disaster and catastrophe. It does not.

Page 57

In each moment of our lives, we make choices about how to relate and react to events and circumstances. We can either choose to succumb to fear, bitterness, disillusionment, resentment and depression, or learn to forgive and heal ourselves.

As I began to understand more clearly the path that had brought me to the doorstep of death, desperation began to set in. Desperation and fear, mostly stemming from the stark realisation that my time was running out. It felt as if I had fallen off the precipice, and was just hanging on by clutching, with both hands, a fragile branch that could snap at any moment.

And the more I thought about this, the more the sense of desperation set in. A desperation based not on a lack of meaning in life – because I could see and feel the love of my family surrounding me – but on the harsh reality of what I had become.

I realised with a sinking feeling that I had lived a life heavily influenced by others. What will others think? I had developed self-doubts and worry about failure, questioning my own abilities, feeling unworthy when good things did happen to me.

I recently came across this quote on Facebook: "When you are 20, you are concerned about what others think of you, when you are 40, you stop caring about what others think of you and when you are 60, you realise that no one was thinking about you in the first place" (Unknown author, Facebook). There was a leather-tanning factory in the town I grew up in. Everybody knew about it because once a day, in late afternoon, it would release these pungent smells – just like rotten eggs – into the air. Years later, to the relief of residents, laws were introduced to force companies to clean pollutants before they were released into the air.

There was a young Sikh man, Dharshan, who worked as a qualified engineer in the tanning factory. He was good at his job, which involved designing and building large, rotating, wooden vats for the treatment of raw hide.

He was the only son and his father had died when he was young. He had been brought up by his mother, who had to really struggle in her life and face a lot of abuse from relatives. Despite all these challenges, she managed to educate he only son to graduate level, and got him married to a very lovely woman, with who he had three children.

They were really doing well until the son began drinking to a point where it became an addiction. He was very close to my parents, and I got to see him in this state several times. He tried many times to overcome this addiction, but to no avail. He was involved in numerous car accidents and altercations. The tanning company did not want to lose his services.

As he began to slide on a downward spiral, with warnings from his employer and failing relationships with his family, the poor man would come to my parents and pour his heart out. He eventually lost his job, and the trust and respect of his family.

He wanted to reverse all that he had done, but felt that he had gone past the point of no return. And, with that, he fell into a state of desperation and depression while his life fell apart. I had just come back from the USA after graduating with an MBA and, as I watched his life unravel, I made a mental note that I would never let my life end up in such a mess.

But it did, because I committed the classic felony of knowing something and not practising it. I call it stubbornness, or pig-headedness, and it is our obsession for permanence and predictability that is the cause of this.

Stubbornness arises from a desire for stability and familiarity. We love to stay put and have everything nailed into place, and fend off anything new or unfamiliar. Yet we know that everything changes, including relationships, aspirations, our bodies, our wealth, feelings, moods...

I am reminded of what Albert Schweitzer, the Nobel Prize winner, once said: "In everyone's life, at some time, our inner fire goes out. It is then burst into flame by an encounter with another human being. We should all be thankful for those people who rekindle the inner spirit."

Ironically, Dharshan was in his element as far as his work was concerned, but his addiction was alcohol. My addiction was my stubbornness to succeed in a wrong choice of career.

It took Dharshan a few years of constant struggle to sort himself out and, eventually, set up his own business. But he was never the same person that he had once been, and his mother, who had struggled as a single parent to nurture and educate him, died a broken soul. His wife and children continued to supported him in his recovery and, over the years, the family became a happier and much more contented unit.

Recalling such personal experiences made me question whether I would ever be able to recover and reverse years of self-afflicted pain and damage. I wanted my life to mean something. I wanted to become the same happy person, full of laughter, life and love, that I had been before.

I didn't want to lose an iota of that and live a compromised life. I knew there would be no second chances, and this was it. I could not afford to let life fly by, as in the past.

We all must find the will to pause and re-examine our everyday actions, and change direction when necessary. Collecting knowledge about things, events, and relationships that affect our lives is important. More important than that is to act upon it.

I had to get rid of these feelings of desperation and fear, and have hope for a better future. It wasn't going to be easy but I knew, deep down, when I looked into the eyes of my wife, that it was not impossible. I knew I had her support.

The healing had begun, but I would need her whole-hearted support. I instinctively knew I had it and could feel it in her presence and manner. It reminded me of what Gloucester, who was blind, said when he was asked on the heath by King Lear, "How do you see the world?" and he simple replied, "I see it feelingly."

I felt a lightness and an urge to shed tears – of what, you may ask? I cannot even begin to describe the feeling in the moment – there was a tinge of sadness, a tinge of happiness, a tinge of nothingness, yet fullness, of quietness – of knowing that, in that moment, nothing mattered but the embrace of love that surrounded me.

In those rare moments, I felt connected to all that was around me, all perfect in their imperfections – no judgements. The Japanese call it wabi-sabi. That moment was raw and simple, and everything made sense, including my own sickness. It is a wonderful way of facing your fears – just accept what is being presented in the moment, without judging it. Fear, after all, is just an emotion.

We all live in constant fear. It is imagined because of how we perceive things as they are now, as they may happen, or past events. Mainly, our fear is that life may not go the way we wish it. What we want to happen may not happen. We want to be in control and to be in charge. We don't want to fail and, in whatever we do – work, relationships, travel, career, meeting our targets, getting old, being alone – there is a fear of the unknown. There is uncertainty. That is our fear. Fear always involves the other; if somebody can take something away from you, it destroys your security. It includes death and illness, work, relationships – they are all the "other". Then fear becomes an underlying feeling that drives our lives.

There is nothing seriously wrong about feeling fear. I know I was stepping out of a life that I could easily have fallen back into. That would have taken no effort but, now that I had looked into the mirror through the eyes of a critic, I certainly had not liked what I had seen.

A number of questions arose in my mind. Had I left it too long? Will my poor health condition hold me back? What was certain was that I would not allow it to stop me from having a go. I knew, if allowed, fear could affect more areas of my life – relationships, health – it would become problematic. Whatever the case, I did want to become a victim of them.

I began by trying to understand the root cause of these fears. Self-doubt, low self-esteem, a sense of hopelessness, powerlessness and ill-health were some of the reasons that popped up. I think it was an important step. I think it helped to identify and be specific about my fears, because it began to provide clues about how I could overcome these fears.

I opened up about these emotions to my wife, and she said I was being too harsh with myself. She said that I should respond to my fears with self-compassion, not impatience and harsh self-criticism. In that way, it would be possible to respond rather than react to whatever challenges came our way.

She said that she believed in me and that she would be there to support me in any way she could. And that she did. A few months after I left the hospital, she found a job – her first job ever – and put me through university, from where I graduated with a Master's degree and a PhD. I can say with full confidence that having the right support can help you overcome fear.

But we should be careful not to allow fear to dominate our thinking and actions. This can stop us from seeing what protection and support we already have. I am reminded of these powerful words by Jeff Warner, a performer/interpreter of traditional music: "We are not put on this earth for ourselves but are placed here for each other. If you are there always for others, then in time of need, someone will be there for you."

The key is to act on a decision and use your self-compassion to get to where you want to. Self-compassion provides you with the courage to overcome your fears. Joyce Marter, a therapist and owner of *Urban Balance*, a counselling practice in the Chicago area, says, "Self-compassion is an essential part of wellness, psychologically, relationally, physically and even spiritually."

Page 63

Dennis Tirch, a psychologist and director of *The Center for Mindfulness and Compassion Focused Therapy*, also comments that self-compassion helps us confront hardships and make beneficial changes in our lives. Self-compassion "allows us to engage our brain and body's basic soothing system."

As you might have noticed in the previous chapters, I got pretty good at self-bashing, or self-criticism. While self-criticism is the preferred path to internal change, we rarely think about showing ourselves kindness. Or, even if we do, we worry that doing so is selfish, complacent, or arrogant.

Gary John Bishop in *Unfu*K Yourself: Get Out of Your Head and into Your Life* writes, "You cannot, I repeat

CANNOT dwell in any blame game in your life. Even blaming yourself is completely useless."

The important point here is that self-compassion can only happen once you stop the self-bashing. Studies carried out by Kristin Neff PhD, associate professor in human development at the University of Texas, in Austin, have shown that self-criticism can lead to lowered self-esteem, anxiety and depression. In short, self-criticism only sabotages us and produces a variety of negative consequences, summarised by Margarita Tartakovsky, Associate Editor, *PsychCentral)* as follows:

"Specifically, according to Neff, 'self-compassion consists of three components. Firstly, self-kindness: being kind, gentle and understanding with yourself when you're suffering. Secondly, common humanity: realizing that you're not alone in your struggles. When we're struggling, we tend to feel especially isolated. We think we're the only ones to experience loss, make mistakes, feel rejected or fail. But it's these very struggles that are part of our shared experience as humans. And, thirdly, mindfulness: observing life as it is, without being judgemental or suppressing your thoughts and feelings.'

"Neff also dispels common myths that may stand in the way of people being kinder to themselves. These include myths about self-compassion being self-pitying, egocentric, or self-indulgent, and the myth that self-criticism is an effective motivator. I would personally say that the last myth has some truth to it – at least to the point where you truly get to grips with your true self or nature.

"Then, and only then, can your healing begin.

"Self-compassion acts like a nurturing parent, Neff says. So, even when you don't do well, you're still supportive and accepting of yourself. Like a kind parent, your support and love are unconditional, and you realize that it's perfectly OK to be imperfect.

"This doesn't mean being complacent. Self-criticism tears us down; it presumes that 'I am bad.' Self-compassion, however, focuses on changing the *behaviour* that's making you unhealthy or unhappy. Neff suggests the following strategies for Self-Compassion.

"Being self-compassionate might seem unnatural at first. These strategies can help. This may be harder for some individuals, particularly if you've experienced trauma, so it's important to work with a therapist.

"First, consider how you'd treat someone else. The simplest thing you can do, according to Neff, is to imagine what you'd do if someone you cared about came to you after failing or getting rejected. What would you say to that person? How would you treat them?

"Secondly, watch your language. You may be so used to criticizing yourself that you don't even realize that you're doing it. So, it helps to pay particular attention to the words you use to speak to yourself. If you wouldn't make the same statements to someone you care about, then you're being self-critical, Neff says.

"Thirdly, comfort yourself with a physical gesture. Kind physical gestures have an immediate effect on our bodies, activating the soothing parasympathetic system. Specifically, according to Neff, physical gestures 'get you out of your head and drop you into your body,' which is important since 'the head loves to run away with storylines.' For instance, she suggests putting your hands over your heart, or simply holding your arm. Any gesture will do.

"Fourthly, memorize a set of compassionate phrases. Whenever you find yourself saying, 'I'm horrible,' it helps to have a few phrases at the ready. Pick statements that really resonate with you. Combining that with a physical gesture — like hands over your heart — is especially powerful, Neff says. She uses the following phrases: *This is a moment of suffering; suffering is part of life; may I be kind to myself in this moment? May I give myself the compassion I need?*

"And, last but not least, practise guided meditation. Meditation helps to retrain the brain and, in this way, self-compassionate gestures and self-soothing become more natural."

These were messages that were echoed in my Sikh faith. I realised, with shame, that I had never really listened to, and practised, the words of wisdom given by the Sikh Gurus.

Never listened to the Guru's words on compassion for oneself and others. The courage to face my worst fears, forgiveness, and much more, if practised, would have provided me with the guidance for everyday living. I had deliberately chosen to become complacent and ignorant. And the reason was simple – I felt in control and successful. Really?

As fear began to fade away into the background, and self-compassion took its place, I began to feel free of my past mistakes and began to look forward to the challenges the future would bring. It felt like I had been given a blank slate to write whatever I wished, without being judged by others. That is what self-compassion does. Each journey begins with you.

You know when people ask you to visualise a favourite place, a beach, a sunset when you are feeling low? Well, that is the moment I think of. The moment I knew I had been given a blank slate – that I had the opportunity to live a meaningful life.

The moment that fear disappeared and the moment that I had finally found the courage to forgive myself, I felt connected to life. It was the moment that my life began to change. I like to call this my moment of awakening. Was it spiritual? Yes, if spirituality is the sense of feeling connected to everything and that connection is love.

These days we read a lot about living in the present moment, in the now, or in this breath. The advice comes from personal development consultants and spiritual gurus. All I needed was a heart attack (warning: don't try this at home - not recommended) to be in the moment, something that we knew instinctively as babies. I had to not only live in the moment, but also make every moment count.

Page 67

Carlos Castaneda, in *Journey to Ixtlan, The Lessons of Don Juan*, puts this in very simple words: "For me the world is weird because it is stupendous, awesome, mysterious, unfathomable; my interest has been to convince you that you must assume responsibility, for being here in this marvellous world, in this marvellous desert, in this marvellous time.

"I want to convince you that must learn to make every act count, since you are going to be here for a very short while, in fact too short for witnessing all the marvels of it."

But you have to be rid of your feelings of self-pity and self-loathing, to be free of any fear and to have self-compassion.

But what about the person who is suffering with you? The person who was with me worried about me, about the future, about the kids, about paying the bills, about leaving the children at home and coming to hospital all day, about an uncertain and unpredictable future, and about what would happen if I died or was incapacitated.

What about her fears of the phone ringing in the middle of the night and her being told I was gone? She must have felt helpless and powerless when she suddenly found herself with a sick husband and three children in a strange, new country.

I know now that it was a very distressing period of anxiety, helplessness and near depression for her. I could see the changes in her physical appearance and the effects of mental torture on her. She wasn't eating well, sleeping well, or taking care of herself.

My illness had triggered distressing emotions in her, but I had been too busy with my own self to even notice, let alone acknowledge this. I didn't realise the damage that my illness was doing to my loved ones.

I would like to say something that is equally important, but usually ignored and not acknowledged. I am guilty about this, too, which is the profound effect that illness has on your nearest and dearest. I can only speak about what I went through and how, from the moment I had the heart attack, it was always about me.

A study published under the title *How Illness Affects Family Members: A Qualitative Interview Survey,* the authors (Eve Wittenberg PhD, Adrianna Saada MPH and Lisa

A Prosser PhD) concluded that "Family members in their sample reported experiencing psychological and non-health effects from having an ill relative, and secondarily somatic effects."

They continue and say that effects on emotional health were most commonly reported as psychological spill-over; non-health effects frequently included changes in daily activities and provision of caregiving.

Spouses of patients reported the broadest range of spill-over domains affected, and adolescents of ill parents the fewest. Family members reported experiencing effects that were perceived as both positive and negative.

Carers experienced a range of difficult emotions. They have to, first and foremost, look after themselves and, secondly, learn the skills to deal with challenges. Then they are in a better position to continue to care for the person in their charge.

Unfortunately, in my case, the sudden nature of my incapacitation did not provide my family the time to prepare for the role of carer. They were thrown in at the deep end. To top it all, we had been in the country for just a few weeks, and all aspects of our lives were in constant flux.

Imagine being in a new country, living with relatives, looking for schools for three children, missing the stability of the life left behind and the uncertainty of finding jobs for financial security. I had always managed my own business, while my wife had dedicated her life to looking after the family.

Throw into the mix the persistent doubts about the wisdom of uprooting the family from a safe and familiar environment, and plunging into uncertainty and chaos.

Deep down, I knew that my wife and children were going through hardships and psychological trauma but, when they were near me, they never showed it.

Yes, guilt set in much later with the realisation about the demands I made, the roles I expected her to play and the responsibilities that she was expected to take up. She had to become the primary provider while I recovered, and she had, up to this point, just been a housewife.

She was expected to take up all these responsibilities. If the roles were reversed, I am pretty sure about what I would have felt and the doubts I would have had.

I saw later how the burden of being the sole caregiver and breadwinner was taking its toll. She always looked tired and emotionally drained as the reversal of roles and responsibilities took their toll. She never complained once, and marched forward with the belief and hope that it would be all good one day.

She has always been more emotionally strong than me. And the children, my two sons and daughter, stepped up too.

I cannot forget the stress, worry and the look of desperation she tried to hide when I was finally transferred to another hospital for an angiogram. She told me later that, as I was being admitted to the ward, a young doctor who had seen my medical reports took her to one side and, in the most unprofessional manner, told her to get her affairs right because the chances of my survival – not recovery – weren't that great.

When she came into the room she was visibly upset, and had been crying. She wouldn't tell me why, because she didn't want me to worry and take on more stress before the procedure. I don't have even half the mettle she has.

She was carrying all this unexpected, extra burden on her shoulders, uncertain about what could happen the next moment, yet walking around as if she didn't have a care in the world. Her whole world had turned upside down.

And there was no one there to tell her that her emotions were valid, and normal, and allowed. And that she didn't have to suffer in silence – she deserved support with these emotions, good and bad. But then, when you are thrown in at the deep end, you are unprepared, and it's only your character at that point that can carry you through.

Fear, loneliness, anxiety, irritability, frustration, guilt, resentment, depression, guilt and embarrassment are some of the emotions that carers go through and have to cope with, according to the *Live-in Care Hub*.

The wellbeing of carers is often overlooked and, mostly, ignored. We take others for granted and expect them to be there for us, no matter what. From what I have gone through and experienced first-hand, it is wise to consider the possibilities of events happening, sometimes unexpectedly, in the future.

They also have fears, and need huge doses of self-compassion in their lives. They need support, too. But, unfortunately, I came to this realisation much later on in my recovery. I had taken the children and my wife for granted. I learnt that we should also build resilience, patience, compassion and patience into our relationships – just as the old adage goes: "In sickness and in health."

I have never met anybody else with such compassion and resilience, who just gets on vigorously with whatever the moment demands of her. All this positive energy that exuded from her gave me strength and the belief that all was going to be well.

We fail to recognise in others the qualities that we seek in ourselves, especially those who are always surrounding us. Somebody recently said that, as you become more proficient in finding positive aspects in other people, you get better at seeing positive aspects of yourself. For this to happen, you have to be engaged in mindful living.

Sounds spot-on, but not easily done. We live in a world of endless distractions, made even more so because of technology. We have become a society of "distraction dependence." We have become less engaged in everyday living. Instead of drifting through life, it's better to live consciously.

Conscious living means having clear goals and pathways. Decisions are made based on conscious choices, and not on external factors and influences on you. This gives you control over your life.

Perhaps it's difficult to see and recognise the obvious. Most likely, we live our lives in a state of unconsciousness. Perhaps we become so obsessed with ourselves that we look for the dramatic, the spectacles in life, rather than being discerning.

That is Chapter 6.

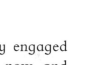

Chapter 6

Conscious Living

Living consciously means being completely engaged with what you are doing in the here and now, and this requires studying and understanding your feelings, beliefs, thoughts and experiences. By using your understanding of yourself to guide your decision-making and control your behaviour, you can transform yourself from reacting to life to responding to it productively instead. Decisions become based, not on habits, but on more conscious thoughts.

Becoming more discerning means questioning your decisions so that you are not falling prey to your old habits but developing new, flexible ones. This is true spontaneity that brings out a better version of yourself. It brings focus, action (as opposed to reaction) and emotional awareness.

In the book, *The Heart of the Soul*, the authors, Gary Zukav and Linda Francis, refer to the recognition and awareness of emotions as physical sensations which they call "emotional awareness." These sensations can be in the throat area, chest, solar plexus, etc. External triggers, such as lack of money, abuse, work and love, activate the emotions within us, and we can learn to recognise them and experience them fully. We should not supress or deny them.

Life, in its simplest form of understanding, is a play or drama. This is the predominant view of most Eastern religions. It's a *"khel", or "tamasha"* in Sikhism, or *"Lila"* or divine play in Hinduism. Aristotle said that the meaning of drama is that it had to have a plot and character development, and you had to see the subtle relationships between plot and character; the thing that would destroy the subtlety was spectacle. We get caught up in the spectacle, rather than weigh things up, consider consequences or alternatives, and really understand the choices we have. This is where we have to learn to be discerning.

My relationships began to take on a new meaning, once I became more conscious of the decisions I was taking. This awareness came with patience and practice. It was very easy to fall back on old habits and react without much thought.

Conscious living shifted me from a life of routines and repetitive, mechanical behaviours, to a life where there was genuine engagement in my relationships. One important point that I noted as I began to live more consciously was that I became less "needy" and enjoyed solitude. We use "alone time" to process our relationships and recalibrate our sense of self. Solitude confirms that we're more than the sum of our reactions to other people and encounters. In solitude, we return to centre. It gives us the chance to take inventory and hear the messages that fill our day. In doing so, we can hone in on what is vital to our wellbeing and what we will take with us to return to the world.

The interesting point to note is that, as I evolved into a more conscious person, the relationships also became a reflection, or measure, of this evolution. This is not so surprising, because no relationship is an end in itself. The evolution of consciousness then allows you to move on, without resorting to the blame game. In other words, there is a natural flow in the relationships and mutual growth.

Conscious living also brings with it inner knowing, or intuition, and this acts as an inner guardian in your relationships. It is something that you can trust, without the mind complicating it, as the "spiritual" inner voice, or non-verbal guidance. From personal experience, the shift in my consciousness caused a shift from being a slave to feelings such as impatience, desperation and frustration, to a state of patience and acceptance.

Page 75

In this state it is easy to let go of that which is not working. I had spent most of my adult life trying to hold onto relationships that were simply toxic. They drained me of so much energy and time. They usually made me feel fear, anxiety and frustration. Now, in a more conscious state, I was the master of, and not slave to, my emotions and thoughts.

Once you truly understand it, you can choose to respond to it instead of reacting to it. Not reacting by working more to get more money, find another partner, lash out, etc., but to respond to the situation from a healthy part of your personality —such as gratitude, contentment, patience and appreciation.

Flourishing Relationships

This is how you challenge the emotion in the moment, not letting the emotion control you, but embracing it, understanding it and responding to it, moving beyond it. Otherwise, you will be overwhelmed by the emotions.

This is how you develop what Gary Zukav, the American spiritual teacher and author, calls mastery of yourself, by moving beyond the control of the external world. On reflection, I knew that I had become an amalgamation of numerous role-playing habits and routines. By learning to break the cycle, the internal talk, the habits, I could finally move with purpose, with consciousness; I could, once again, learn to stay put and be steadfast, no matter what.

Read, talk to people and go places where your evolution is reinforced. For me it was poetry, such as *Desiderata*, a 1927 prose poem by the American writer, Max Ehrmann. It is a long poem, and this is an extract. It says, "Go placidly amid the noise and haste and remember what peace there may be in silence. As far as possible, without surrender, be on good terms with all persons. Speak your truth quietly and clearly; and listen to others, even to the dull and ignorant; they too have their story." Reading this pulled me back when I felt my discipline slip.

My acceptance of my new, changed situation, including the emotions that came with it, provided ample opportunity – even under the most difficult circumstances – to add a deeper meaning to my life. I was convinced that my best days were yet to come. What a wonderful freedom it was to discover that I could choose my own meaning, and that meaning would keep me filled with life.

My relationships changed dramatically, too, and a sense of constant peace and contentment followed. It didn't feel as if I were pushing against opposing forces but, rather, flowing with it. And I got to travel to different countries in the word to present papers and projects, and to attend conferences.

I truly believed I had a better future, a future that I could dream, design and build. I was not going to wallow in self-pity and just go around in circles, complaining and waiting for the next heart attack. I had confronted death face-to-face, and I didn't like what I had seen.

The more I examined my feelings and experiences, the more I developed faith and hope in myself and the future. This gave me the courage and tenacity to stand up and face my suffering head-on, and the mess I had made of my life. I was not going to allow myself to decline further. It is surprising what strength faith, especially spiritual faith, can give you.

Page 77

I know it is true – I am the living proof. Surviving and really living a life of joy and contentment after over 20 years of being diagnosed with critical heart failure. Still getting stronger too, if I may add, without any attempt whatsoever of tempting fate.

There was a journey I had to take to get to this point. What does it actually mean to live consciously? I have, and I am pretty sure that you must have, at one point or another in your lives, come to the realisation that we pretty much have become creatures of habits, routines and patterns.

Every aspect of our lives has, beneath the surface, a set process that keeps us supposedly sane. And this includes constantly having an internal conversation.

This provides a constant reassurance that all is well in the world.

Part of the problem is that we come to see the world as either this or that. Referred to as polar or dual thinking, it involves reasoning involving extremes or opposites.

Our language is one of duality and, often, things appear to be mutually exclusive, when, in fact, they are not. Instead of looking at these abstractions as mutually exclusive, instead try to see them as inextricably bound and one. Alan Watts, a philosopher who popularised Eastern philosophy, calls this "polar unity" – seeing the foreground with the background.

We create problems in our minds with dualistic comparisons, and this invariably leads to unreasonable expectations, especially in relationships. Too much A, not enough B. But, with correct practice – please allow me to use the word meditation – duality, that seemed like a problem before, becomes perfectly fine as it is.

In being able to do so, I learned to live, not in despair or suffering, but looking for meaning from whatever presents itself in the moment. Not to pursue expectations in my relationships, but to let them ensue as and when they do. And that is a profound discovery that guides me in everyday living. Giving love, happiness, relationships and "things" room to breathe and come to me.

Realising that, although you are taught to choose one from the other, the world has many views, and you are not restricted to seeing them one at a time. Living more consciously frees you to see and feel that there is a natural flow between what we perceive as opposites.

And it is this change in thinking that provides resilience in your relationships. In short, you appreciate and learn to see the ups and downs – the waves – as an integral aspect of all relationships.

But it is important to face yourself with honesty about knowing yourself. With our habit of rationalising all our actions, it takes boldness and determination to deconstruct and unpack the ideas that form the complex web of perceptions and ideas we have about ourselves.

The aim should be to develop a clearer understanding of what really makes you tick. And it is this understanding that allows you to make changes in the way you think and perceive. Living consciously means seeing the natural flow of events and moments, and allowing yourself to flow with them. Then, your authentic and spontaneous self presents itself.

You will agree that not everyone can understand you, especially your deeper nature and qualities. There are only a few who can relate to you. But, on a more positive note, it's my observation that more and more people are now consciously exploring their own inner selves. The right questions are being asked. There seems to be a shift from total materialism and self-focus to finding pathways for more meaningful living.

Living more consciously also meant that I was no longer trying to have many friends. I did not want to win favour amongst many friends, because I knew that it meant that I was accommodating myself to their expectations. I wanted to be loved and accepted for who I was. It is important that we honour our true, deeper nature, otherwise we are just resisting or denying ourselves.

As I began living more consciously, the criteria for my relationships changed. I sought honesty, deeper values, integrity, sincerity and clarity. A far cry from my previous "life", where relationships were mostly transactional. Living consciously increases our capacity to love, because we seek deeper connections. We are not living at the surface, but much deeper down.

Everybody knows the old adage that beauty is only skin-deep. When you begin to live consciously you are not swayed by beauty or charm, but use a deeper awareness. I began to see such qualities as superficial, because you are listening for something deeper in yourself, and in others, too. I stopped judging and comparing and, instead, began to see and hear from a deeper place. The relationships became more than a conversation. Instead, they became more like a warm embrace, where more is shared with ease. Or, in simpler language, your relationships become more synchronised, perhaps because you have a deeper sense of purpose and destiny.

Surviving the heart attack convinced me that I had a greater destiny in the world, and that my relationships would also form a part of that destiny. Together, these would play a significant role in the unfolding and expression of my life.

And this brings me to a very important point. Relationships that have meaning and last are built with deep understanding and commitment. Otherwise, you will not find what you are looking for in one another, because you are simply not looking for the right things. This is one reason that we get stuck in relationships that feel like a trap from which we cannot free ourselves easily.

By being more discerning, you can avoid being attracted by meaningless things, being seduced by others, or going into a relationship because you felt lonely and there was nothing better. You will not find a real connection with another if you are not discerning, because these meaningless things do not speak of greater purpose or destiny in life. They are momentary and, as such, will only lead to disillusionment and disappointment.

Of course, there are other relationships that do not require you to give away yourself. These can be at work, or simple companionships. People who keep you connected to everyday living.

When you want to go into a serious relationship, and you meet that someone special who feels just right, then you must very carefully consider if you are both ready for this. Get to know their values, lifestyle and traits, and see if there is compatibility between you. Then allow the relationship to form, and commit to it every day. In this way, it will be sustained and benefit both of you.

A word of caution here. You should not try to change somebody to make them compatible. If you do, then the relationship is doomed to fail. You will have wasted time and energy to make something work that just does not work. Yes, when you are compatible there is growth and learning for both.

There are many lessons to learn in discernment, and the best way is to practise them. To walk on the path with acute senses that evaluate and educate you, teaches you what is true and what is not. To see real beauty that is deep and everlasting. See, feel, hear, smell and notice (to understand) that which is taking you to your greater purpose. You will begin to see how invaluable this is, and how it was missing in your previous way of living and decision-making.

I truly believe that our inner spirit is here to take us somewhere. It is providing us with experiences to show us what is real and what is not. I am determined not to be distracted from this discovery, no matter in what form it comes – seduction, beauty, wealth, or charm. I am now mature and strong enough to engage with life, knowing that I have a greater destiny to fulfil. And, importantly, share this destiny with people who are spontaneous and authentic.

If you are not, then you will end up being a people-pleaser, never speaking up and voicing your true opinion, out of fear of not being liked or not pleasing others. You will constantly compare yourself to others and say things to yourself, like, "She's smarter than me," or, "They are so much more creative than me," or, "He can do it better than me." Not being spontaneous and authentic also means that you feel the need to constantly follow the rules. You do what you think you *should* do, not always what you *want* to do. In fact, you may not even know what you *want*, and you feel the constant need to strive for perfection and for your life to appear perfect. Worse still, you might work all the time and not take time for yourself. You think you need to constantly work to prove yourself and to live up to the expectations of others. Your work defines you. You are burnt-out, or at the brink of burn-out.

The choice is yours.

Then, and only then, can you see that every relationship is a gift of love.

This is Chapter 7.

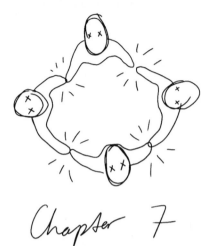

Chapter 7

Relationships As Gifts Of Love

This book is about how relationships give us the gift of love. How this love is visible, daily. How it helps us to rise to the world and live our best life possible. How relationships can serve – help – us in what we want to do, as guides for us in doing the things we need and, sometimes, in doing things that we did not even know we could do.

However difficult life may be, in *One Small Step Can Change Your Life: The Kaizen Way*, author Robert Maurer reminds us that the solution is often found in the scariest of places: "When life gets scary and difficult, we tend to look for solutions in places where it is easy or at least familiar to do so, and not in the dark, uncomfortable places where real solutions might lie."

They say hindsight is a wonderful teacher, insofar as it gives you clarity of mind to see the past in a new light. As I reflect for a moment about all the people who have crossed my path, the relationships and experiences I have had, all my moods and the seasons I have experienced, I can come to only one conclusion: nothing is permanent, everything changes and is in flux. If only I could anchor myself in that which never changes, I would be happy.

This was not far from the truth, as I came to discover later. In fact, that was the secret to all relationships, to anchor oneself in the safest harbour there is, a harbour in your heart. As the Buddha said, "Your work is to discover your world and then with all your heart give yourself to it."

We have created smokescreens and lost our anchor because of storms created by our thoughts, beliefs and perceptions. These are just manifestations of the mind, our thoughts, rather than from the deep core within us.

It is the basis of the personal image we build about ourselves, of who we think we are. It can also be called the personal ego. And it stops us from seeing the whole picture – just like a horse with its blinkers, that limit its vision into one narrow tunnel. Ego is another word for tunnel vision - narrow-mindedness.

Anchoring required, as a very first step, the removal of the smokescreens I had created around myself. In the journey of life, I had developed thoughts, prejudices, beliefs and perceptions that had taken me further away from my true calling in life. When the mind is absorbed in excessive thought, it is difficult to find your way, given the cloud of distorted thinking.

I had chosen a path in life based on short-term gains, reassuring myself that I would always be able to find a way back to my core passion in life. I eventually got locked into an uncontrollable spiral of events and circumstances that made me forget not only the way back, but also what I had been born to do.

Not only had I had lost my way, but I had also ignored the gift of service to others that I had been born with. It is H.G. Wells who said, "Losing your way on a journey is unfortunate. But, losing your reason for the journey is a fate crueller." Losing your way is attributed to losing sight of your core purpose, a sensation accompanied by emptiness and confusion.

If you are feeling lost, reconnect with your purposeful self to get back on track. It may require you to get quiet to listen to the stillness within that knows your next move. To concede defeat may be your best move, and not as detrimental as you might think. In surrendering, you are made aware of a new direction you hadn't considered before. I had ended up completely hypnotised by material acquisitions, and this had set the stage for the same old same old. Physical things had become more important than feelings of goodwill. My thinking had become distorted in a world I saw as competitive and governed by the principle of cause and effect. I had, in a sense, lost touch of the fact that all things had meaning and were connected to each other.

I had made concessions by losing moral grounds and rationalising that others do it too, and they seemed successful and happy. I had become preoccupied with future expectations and had lost touch with reality. I believed that everything, relationships included, could be measured and quantified.

In short, I had lost my sense of what was reality and what was make-believe. You get stuck in making plans for today and tomorrow, without grasping the reality of your world. A world of meaningless repetition, habits and uncertainty. I had been caught and trapped in storms created on a path I was not meant to walk.

Tony Fahkry, a self-empowerment author, offers the following advice; "Although it may not appear that way, contained within uncertainty lies the opportunity to reconnect with your intuitive compass." Contained within each uncertainty lies the opportunity to step into your own power and know your true worth. Don't allow it to be obscured by opposing what tomorrow will bring.

He continues, "Whilst we're endowed with intuitive guidance by way of emotions, many are less inclined to heed the messages. This is because they are busy attending to the torrents of emotions that being lost invokes." You have to trust that you will reach your destination before long.

"You just have to let things be and not do anything about them. That is probably the greatest discipline in the world because our whole thing is about making it happen. The point is to be present and trust the process," write authors Charlene Belitz and Meg Lundstrom, in *The Power of Flow: Practical Ways to Transform Your Life with Meaningful Coincidence.* Every relationship creates its own emotional language, which either deepens with time or just fades away. I quantified the time and effort spent on the relationship and, unwittingly, made demands based on my personal expectations of the relationships.

Page 87

I set up rules for the relationships, and didn't hesitate to bring these up when I felt they had been bent or broken. And I held the other to account, rarely considering the other's perspective. I was too busy validating my version of the relationship.

This probably happened because my first love was, in the end, rejected. According to Savannah Grey, a hypnotherapist, when we get rejected, treated poorly, or someone blows hot and cold in a relationship with us, we often become stuck and fixated on that person. We become convinced that we're in love and we try, over and over again, to prove ourselves, to show the object of our affection that we are worthy of their love and attention.

We often don't recognize that the reason someone isn't interested in us may have absolutely nothing to do with us at all. We tend to internalize the rejection; that it must be because we've been seen, evaluated and judged as not good enough, and that they are no longer interested.

And we spend a lot of time to get them interested. It's called the "I want you because you don't want me" syndrome. It is said, "The best way to make a girl fall in love with you is to ignore her." Sad, but true. Why do we do this? What is it about us that makes us chase after someone who ignores us, treats us poorly, or flat-out doesn't want us?

Is it because, if we actually get them to change their minds about us, then that somehow proves our worth? What, do we then get to say, "See, I am awesome. I told you I was right about me." It sounds ridiculous, but isn't that what we're really doing?

When we look to others to show us our worth, Sara continues, they are always going to fall short. Primarily, because it's no one else's job to give us our self-esteem – that's our job. Secondly, people are mostly self-interested; they don't care about how you feel about you – the fact that you are jumping through hoops and treating them like they are the greatest thing since sliced bread is a huge ego boost for them, and you gaining self-respect changes the dynamics of the relationship. When you stop jumping, it doesn't serve them and they don't want that, so they will deliberately, or inadvertently, behave in a manner that keeps you stuck and fixated on them.

When we have low self-esteem, we have become so comfortable with our own negative thoughts and beliefs about ourselves that we will actually seek out people and situations that confirm those beliefs. It's the devil we know, and it feels familiar and like home. We have become so used to the idea that love equals pain, and that what we are calling love is actually us seeking validation and begging to have someone show us our worth.

If someone healthy, who was interested in us and was offering us the relationship that we claim we want, did show up in our lives, we would run like hell, because it goes against everything that we believe about ourselves and we would feel incredibly uncomfortable. So, instead, we inadvertently seek out people who evoke those feelings of unworthiness in us.

Page 89

The problem is, when someone can't make up their mind about us, the price we pay in trying to convince them that we're good enough is our self-esteem. The mere fact that we are going to all this effort proves to them that we actually aren't worthy because, if we were, we would know our own worth and we would've told them to take a hike long ago.

When you engage with a fence-sitter, or continue in a relationship with someone who treats you poorly, you will find that there is always another obstacle, another reason why they can't give you the relationship you want. You pay the price, and the pay-off for you is that you get to continue to confirm to yourself that you aren't good enough. You will end up feeling used and like you are just someone's option for a rainy day.

It becomes a never-ending cycle, and you may go from relationship to relationship and find yourself in the same situation, with the same guy, who just happens to have a different face.

When you realize that you determine your worth, that you deserve more than just crumbs of someone's attention, and when you treat you in a loving, respectful way, others will follow your lead. You teach people how to treat you, to start treating you right. When you change the way that you feel about you, you will stop seeking validation and relationships from unwilling sources.

Healthy people don't sit around wondering why someone doesn't want them. They are too busy living their lives... next.

I had perhaps taken that rejection too personally. It had changed something inside me and I wanted to never feel vulnerable and at the mercy of another. Perhaps the need to control came from there.

I wanted to be in charge and control the other, and knew that this was driven by fear. Fear that gradually developed because I had stepped onto the wrong path. I had forgotten to be forgiving and compassionate. I had failed to learn to use words and actions that made love sacred.

How could I then have experienced my relationships as gifts of love, when I had been too busy managing and manipulating them?

Master Oogway , in the movie *Kung Fu Panda*, remarks, "Yesterday is history, tomorrow is a mystery, and today is a gift... that's why they call it present." I had to lay to rest my past and the near-death experience; I had certainly developed in myself an awareness and deep appreciation of the present moment.

I had to begin with forgiveness. I knew intuitively that, by embracing forgiveness, I could once again get hope, gratitude and joy. By letting go of grudges and bitterness, I could make room for healthier relationships. To forgive myself and those that I had erred against and hurt in the past.

Please indulge me for a moment for a second quote by the soothsayer in *Kung Fu Panda 2*; "Your story may not have such a happy beginning, but that does not make you who you are, it is the rest of it - who you choose to be."

I would encourage everyone to watch more children's cartoons to get real knowledge – I do. I must admit to shedding a few tears when Simba tries in vain to rouse his father, King Mufasa, in *The Lion King*. As I said before – watch cartoons. They will change you for ever.

Forgiveness is the first step towards healing. You harden your hearts when you fail to forgive yourselves of your own pain. Lying in hospital, the self-pity turned into personal loathing. I felt a deep sense of anger at who I had become.

I had lost the fun and caring of myself, my natural beingness, and had replaced it with this hard, cold-hearted person whom I would have hardly recognised if he had stood right in front of me.

I was 39 years old. I had already lived a chunk of my life. I could visibly see the pain in my wife's and children's faces. Faces that I had not really seen before, with expressions that spoke of the pain of the past years yet were filled overflowing love for me. Faces that had seen lots of affection expressed through gifts and luxuries, but not given enough love. God, I really hated myself in that moment. Deep, personal pain can take you either into a deep cesspit with little hope of return, or to a place of self-reflection that can lead you to recovery. You could also linger in between these two extremes when you are still emotionally confused, unstable, or disturbed about your current situation.

In that moment I was overwhelmed with gratitude that the very people whom I had hurt were reciprocating with gifts of love. And that is when I consciously made the choice to pick myself up and put the past behind me. I wanted to be like them, and they were here with me right now and forever, saying "We are here for you; we love you; we want to share your pain and we want you to be whoever you choose to be. But please don't give up; don't die; we need you."

I, too, wanted to give them gifts of love.

Stephen Levine, an American poet and writer best known for his work on death, eloquently puts it this way: "Personal pain is unbearable but if you make it THE pain in your heart, it can then be shared by the heart of common experience, the heart of all of common experience, the heart of all. Genuine healing occurs when we take ourselves mercifully into our own hearts and accept the totality of our lives."

Before the heart attack, I had experienced the attention given to success and had loved to bask in these praises. We love attention. We love the relationships that come with the attention. But today, in hospital, I was reminded that there is no love without selflessness.

As I examined my feelings of success, my "highs", more closely, I sadly realised that these feelings of love were based on selfishness. My own desires had made me self-centred and focused on self-interest.

I had to seek my inner spirit that, my Sikh Gurus had reminded me, time and again, pervaded in all. To know that everyone sought to be loved and cared for. To know that the only way that my relationships would ooze with the warmth of love was to be love itself.

I know this might sound like a romantic and unrealistic aim, but I am convinced that reconnecting with your spirit brings you a deep sense of contentment and compassion in whatever presents itself in the moment. even the Bible speaks of the sacrament of the present moment, or the concept of Ichi Go Inchi E, which translates as "this moment exists only now and won't come again."

We are all connected to a greater intelligence through intuition and emotional guidance. Whilst you may veer off-course you can never stray far, because your connection to this intelligence is far greater than any other connection you have ever experienced.

It is a place where all judgements and criticisms stop, and all that remains is a sense of wonder at how your life flows naturally when unhindered by your personal boundaries and limitations. You realise that life is a wonder and mystery.

If I could choose a single word to describe this, it would be "trust". Trusting that, in every moment, you are being taken care of no matter what. Perhaps trust and faith mean the same thing if taken in the right context. Perhaps not.

What do I mean by trust? Trust is an awareness that life will continue to have meaning and beauty, even amidst darkness and suffering. Trust is an attitude of hopefulness about life, a sense that the power of love is the greatest power, at least over the long haul.

Trust is a conviction that we, ultimately, can experience something deep in all of us that connects all of us and is bigger that the image we have about ourselves.

And relationships are built on trust. Trust gives meaning, hopefulness and beauty to life. Just as life is fluid, trust can be, too. Reconnecting with your spirit takes you to a place of trust.

It takes time and effort to build trust, and we need to have faith that it will last. But, when distrust creeps in, our relationships suffer, and we lose faith.

I learnt that spiritual growth requires leaps of faith. As the Indian poet, musician and artist, Rabindranath Tagore, so eloquently expressed it; "Faith is a bird that feels dawn breaking and sings while it is still dark."

Faith requires complete trust; trust that life will continue to have meaning and beauty, amidst darkness and suffering.

It requires teamwork. And my family was my first team and we were going to place our trust and faith in our Gurus to lead us to live a life that would be fulfilling, both to us and those we met.

Before all these positive things could happen, there was this underlining fear that gripped me. It felt almost as if I were being suffocated by it. Where does fear stem from? And the only short answer I could get was - uncertainty. Uncertainty in my abilities to cope with this situation. Uncertainty arising from perceived personal weaknesses. Uncertainty arising from inadequate information, experience, wisdom. Fear arising from holding on to things, events and relationships. Fear arising from the past I had created and the stark consequences of that.

Was I going to let uncertainty hold me back? And what could I do about it? How could I believe in myself again? How could I overcome my fear and have the courage to face each moment with calm and pragmatism?

The gurus call it the pragmatic mind, *babake buddhi*, as opposed to the limiting, psychological mind. The only way to get over the fear was to let go of all that had brought me to this point in my life.

I asked myself what I would ask for if I found a genie magic lamp which offered three wishes. Even that confused me, and fear took over again. The "clever" psychological mind was taking over, considering "what-if" scenarios. Which wish, granted, would bring multiple rewards? I found myself drifting back to my old self.

And that is how life, minus the magic lamp, works. All our efforts concentrated in trying the find the elusive reward. Always searching. And the same is true for relationships and, when found, always expecting and demanding more. Never satisfied.

My Guru reminded me of the genie within all of us. Always ready to grant unlimited wishes and, just like in the fable, I had to clean the lamp of the dust that I had collected on my poor soul to release the genie of compassion and love within me.

The teachings of my Gurus guide me gently to clear the smoke and re-anchor myself through simple teachings, such as the practice of being compassionate to others (and the environment); treating everyone with love and respect; being patient and understanding; and of listening and responding with language that lifts and lightens.

I was reminded about what I had always known - the door to my happiness was within me. And, to know this, I had been guided to embark on this journey. In Paulo Coelho's book *The Alchemist*, Santiago, the young shepherd-boy, traverses the globe in search of his personal legend, only to find it was present at home all along. Had he not embarked upon the journey, he would have missed the wisdom and insights gained along the way.

I am also reminded of these few lines by the poet, T. S. Elliot:

"We shall not cease from exploration
And the end of all our exploring
Will be to arrive where we started
And know the place for the first time."

This four-line summary, according to Jordan Peterson, a psychologist and author of the *12 Rules for Life*, is the most remarkable elaboration of the relationship between individual consciousness and the reality itself.

And there is nothing external that can bring you this joy. I learnt that, rather than analyse everything, every event, or situation, I just needed to pause and practise these teachings to rediscover the fountain of love that I, and you, have always had within us.

To allow my intentions, attention and actions to be the same. Then this light, or love connection, that has always been inside you, becomes the guide again.

Alice Koller, author of the book *An Unknown Woman* (1982), exploring the philosophical and psychological issues of self-identity, expressed the following: "I've arrived at this outermost edge of my life by my own actions.

"Where I am, is thoroughly unacceptable. Therefore, I must stop doing what I've been doing. This had to be my very first step towards recovery."

All spiritual teachings point out, time and again, that the cause of human suffering is the illusion that we are what we associate with, do, or think. We attach our mind and body to events, feelings and objects as if they are central to our existence.

We know they are transient and do not need to control our lives but, still we put our faith in them, even when they lead us to inevitable disappointment.

Our culture, religion, friends, society, family, education, all contribute to our beliefs and perceptions. If we lose our connection with this timeless and universal part of us – love – we live as victims to the changing winds of life; never realising that it is the love inside us and between us that has been constant, brought us here, and kept suffering at bay.

Keeping that connection tunes us, like a musical instrument, to have a clearer perception and to see beyond physical associations on to what helps our deeper being and soul, so that we can live by associating with the protective, compassionate, nurturing and constant divine light within us.

We make decisions about everything. This process begins the moment we open our eyes in the morning. Perhaps five more minutes of sleep. Every breath driven by a process. Until we go to sleep. Decision-making gives us a sense of control, self-importance, of being confident and being sure of our chosen path.

That is how we have been conditioned to do things. There must be a framework, a process, or method to achieve a goal. The goal is in the future, and we must take steps to take us from here to there. And we take relationships the same way.

Often, we strategize on this, with subtle manipulation replacing spontaneity. Happiness being sought and not experienced in the moment. Everything planned to the minutest detail, with timeframes to match. We intellectualise everything we do, and logically reason things.

The teachings of the masters provide pointers on how to break this limiting, archetypal thinking and begin to live a life of spontaneity. It begins with listening, and there are two ways to listen: with the intellect, or with the heart.

When the intellect listens, there is always a dichotomy: it thinks in terms of right/wrong, correct/incorrect, believable/unbelievable. The intellect never goes beyond the personal image we have created about ourselves.

It looks upon the heart as insane, and never trusts it. The heart has almost been smothered because it cannot be trusted. You never know when it might make you do things you'll have to pay for later.

That brings me back to the second way of listening, and that is through the heart. This requires trust. What do I mean by trust? Trust is an awareness that life will continue to have meaning and beauty, even amidst darkness and suffering.

Trust is an attitude of hopefulness about life, a sense that the power of love is the greatest power, at least over the long haul. Trust is a conviction that we, ultimately, can experience our true nature, which is compassionate and forgiving.

Without trust, no amount of techniques, disciplines, retreats, or spiritual directors, or any other kind of effort or struggle, will result in on-going encouragement and vitality.

I had to take responsibility for my actions and offload the heavy baggage I carried on my shoulders. Consciously and slowly, I gradually let go of my anger, judgements, jealousies, labelling and attachments.

I stopped analysing and paid less attention to the constant internal talk. I had to trust that life would take care of me if I could let go of my sense of control and let it.

All the teachings pointed to emptying the mind. To empty my vessel so that love could fill it again. Be the awareness and be attentive in every moment. Surrender to the present moment, where problems do not exist. It is here that you experience pure joy and are able to embrace your true selves (light).

Anchor yourself here. I came across the teachings of Lao Tzu, Tao Te Ching that really moved me: "Simplicity, patience, compassion. These three are your greatest treasures. Simple in actions and thoughts, you return to the source of being.

"Patient with both friends and enemies, you accord with the way things are. Compassionate toward yourself, you reconcile all beings in the world."

Gradually, I stopped being a performer (living a life of concepts), and began to anchor myself in a place deep within myself that felt calm and unconflicted. I began to feel at peace. I was free from the past.

Knowing your inner self requires a high level of introspection and self-awareness, and herein lies the challenge. We look outside to find answers to what is inside. If you misplace your car-keys in the house, do you go outside on the streets to look for them? Sounds foolish, doesn't it?

Stress and anxiety are in abundance in our lives. Stressful circumstances and pressures abound. So many things in life irritate us, provoke us, frustrate us, exasperate us and, every time we feel like we're just about ready to "enjoy some peace and quiet," something else happens and, once again, peace is but a delusion.

And this will the norm if you do not anchor yourself in the special place inside you.

By anchoring yourself in this special space, you can follow-through your actions and play the hand you have been dealt with grace and acceptance. You become grateful for all your experiences and emotions (fear, joy, love, adventure, loss) and become creative, trusting that your chosen path is full of fleeting experiences and emotions.

You begin to live in a "space" where these experiences and emotions take place, yet remain unaffected, in peace and without fear. "You owe success and happiness solely to yourself. So why not make your inner self proud of your daily decisions and actions?" writes Edmond Mbiaka, a self-help writer.

We have all gone on a trip, a holiday, a visit to a favourite place — places we enjoy, to relax and be happy. But, after some time, we want to be back in the comfort of our own home. Anchoring yourself is very similar, a return to your true home, the self, to enjoy the comforts of your home (respect, love, steadfast, understanding, patience, forgiving, non-judgemental).

And you will discover something that never changes in you. It has always been the awareness, detached from all that is happening around or to you. Beyond your identity, your name, your work, the roles you play.

That is who you are - your true home. Anchor yourself there and constantly maintain the connection (to your inner space, the spirit) through meditation.

I think these words by the Ponca Chief, White Eagle, convey a powerful message that provides guidance on the importance of anchoring yourself in a safe port: "When you are in doubt, be still, and wait; when doubt no longer exists for you, then go forward with courage.

"So long as mists envelop you, be still; be still until the sunlight pours through and dispels the mists -- as it surely will. Then act with courage."

It's when you become anchored in your true spirit that you begin to recognise and value your inner beauty and, when you do, it has a dramatic effect on your relationships.

That is Chapter 8.

Chapter 8

Value Inner Beauty

This chapter is about going beyond the superficial and connecting with your inner beauty, characterised by unconditional love and kindness. This has a profound effect on relationships. We begin to see relationships as inextricably bound – as connected.

We move beyond duality. Duality is simply defined as a tendency to live in confusion and insecurity because of lack of clarity about which path of life to choose. When we are unsure about who we are, the choices we make reflect that uncertainty.

While our outer appearances change, our inner beauty lasts a lifetime. That is where our value lies, and that is how we can hold on to and have great relationships.

This chapter is also about the subtleties of relation-ships. In other words, there is more meaning behind the stated words and gestures that has not been stated, between yourselves. Nobody else understands it.

It is the subtleties expressed through gestures, a light touch, a smile, a look, or a twitch of the nose, and unstated words that provide the depth of love in relationships. The subtleties develop when there is trust, gratitude, faith and love in relationships.

It is the lack of effort and understanding that we put in our own self which leads to the pain of failed relationships. Our knowledge about ourselves is incomplete and yet we attempt, time and again, to enter various relationships, with the same result.

Though we may keep a little quiet about this, especially when we're young, we tend, deep down, to be rather hopeful that we will – eventually – manage to find a secure and, ideally, harmonious relationship, deeply fulfilling work, a happy family life and the respect of others.

Page 104

But life has a habit of dealing us a range of blows, and we are left damaged. I had learnt, over the months after the heart attack, to value these fragments. Over the centuries, Zen masters developed an argument that pots, cups and bowls that had become damaged shouldn't simply be neglected or thrown away.

They should continue to attract our respect and attention, and be repaired with enormous care – this process symbolising a reconciliation with the flaws and accidents of time, reinforcing some big, underlying themes of Zen. The word given to this tradition of ceramic repair is kintsugi: Kin = golden, tsugi = joinery.

In an age that worships youth, perfection and the new, the art of kintsugi retains a particular wisdom – as applicable to our own lives as it is to a broken teacup. The care and love expended on the shattered pots should lend us the confidence to respect what is damaged and scarred, vulnerable and imperfect – starting with ourselves and those around us.

All those broken relationships teach us something about ourselves and, if we can pick up the pieces and join them with love and reflection, the outcome is a stark realisation that our present outlook on life is made much richer because of, and not in spite of it.

Applying the principle of kintsugi to your broken or damaged relationships provides not only learning but also understanding, compassion and forgiveness. It brings your closer to your own vulnerability and beauty of the heart.

We can also learn a lot from nature. Nature is so reliable and resilient. No matter the conditions, it always manages to share its beauty. From Japanese aesthetics, the concept of Wabi suggests a sort of amazing, eternal reliability of nature that continues to survive, no matter what humans do. It exhibits a sort of everlasting sanity. Just like a weed that persistently appears in the cracks of concrete, no matter how hard you try to get rid of it. It's always finding a way to survive and pass its resilient nature on to the next plant. That is real power. No matter the odds, you still come out fighting and stand tall.

Page
105

I had to be the same – no matter the challenges, I could not ever entertain any thoughts of giving up, and embraced uncertainty, fearlessly and confidently. I had faced myself with stark honesty, and now had the power to choose and write my own story as I wished.

The writer and author Salman Rushdie provides these powerful words: "Those who do not have power over the story that dominates their lives, power to retell it, rethink it, deconstruct it, joke about it, and change it as times change, truly are powerless, because they cannot think new thoughts."

If I wanted ownership of my own story, I had to learn to accept the imperfections of my life and start recognising and appreciating the flow of life that I was born to live before I got waylaid. To become grounded once again.

It would not be an easy task, but I knew it had to be done. I was not going to plunder my second chance to really live. I am reminded of what William Blake said; "If a fool would persist in his folly, he would become wise." I had to make the change, and wise up. Everything depended on it.

I realised I had a long journey ahead, but was determined to embark on it no matter the cost. I had to. There wasn't any other option. I had found the one most powerful reason to survive the heart attack. It was the right reason, with the right intent.

I was no longer dependent on some concept or thought that made me feel safe in my head. I didn't need to feel empty any more. The fact that I had survived such a traumatic event was proof that life could be resilient.

We create our sense of "beingness" from ideas. Ideas shaped by our thoughts and experiences of the past and present, and perceptions of the future. Friendships and relationships provide validation. These ideas make us feel secure in ourselves but, when we are proven wrong we fall apart, feeling helpless and limited. These ideas translate into our psychological make-up. They impact upon how we live, our relationships, thoughts and moods. Our perceptions, perspectives and expectations.

The point is that the behavioural aspect of a person's psychological makeup relates to the elements that motivate actions or cause reactions. We are all looking for success, happiness, love, stability. We face many challenges and struggles on the way. We spend most of our time concentrating on the end of the journey. Often frustrated with the journey itself. The journey is as important as the destination.

I had begun to discover the sense of 'beingness' – of not being in conflict with my outside world and finding, outside, what nurtured and developed me inside. I had begun to live a life with a sense of presence and not as a pre-programmed, robotic human – human robot. I was consciously working on my "beingness", using practices such as meditation, and keeping the company of others seeking the same inner self. The information and knowledge we feed our mind, and the company we keep, have a direct relationship to how we live our lives.

Yes, I still got, and get, emotional. Emotions, after all, are meant to fluctuate, just like your blood pressure is meant to fluctuate. It's a system that's supposed to move back and forth, between happy and unhappy. That's how the system guides you through the world, writes the American social psychologist and writer, Daniel Gilbert.

I began to learn to separate the emotions from that one aspect of me that never changes. Learning to be an observer, rather than the participant. I was reaching a stage of letting go all the things that were holding me down – in short, letting go of the idea I had built of myself. The personal image I had created of myself.

Alan Watts says, "Get to know yourself and let go of all beliefs and ideas of who you are. Don't hang on to anything — even God (because if you believe in it you are making it a thing to hang onto; so in a way a belief in God is a lack of faith because if you are still clinging you do not have faith because faith is a state of total let go)."

He continues, "Once you get to a stage of let go you don't need anything to hang on to because there is no need for it whatsoever. Because you have crossed from one shore to the other and you don't need the raft anymore. Get off — leave the raft behind. How things feel is the way you are. Instead of looking for the ideal place — relationship — is simply to be it!"

I consciously, but gradually, moved away from the habit of determining my own worth (value) by how everybody around me behaved or reacted to me. This was such a liberating experience — not being on my toes all the time and constantly seeking the approval of others. I could now put my past behind me and acknowledge that the real essence of my beingness had never been lost. It had just become covered by layers of misjudgements, wrong decisions, and the choice of wrong paths that had resulted in unbearable pain. Pain that had disguised itself as some sort of deluded, personal achievement.

Every step that had led me to this sorry state had underlying tones of conditional demands — both conscious and unconscious. But now I could see that, stripped of all these delusions, I still was the same person who had a passion for life before getting waylaid. I could feel and see my inner soul in all its beauty and love. This was an important realisation towards experiencing the beauty of each relationship. I began to get glimpses of myself in others, and them in me. No more fear, but acceptance of the relationship as it presented itself to me.

I love the words by the writer, Ritu Ghatourey: "Love is what we were born with. Fear is what we learned here. The spiritual journey is the relinquishment or unlearning of fear and the acceptance of love back in our hearts."

I learnt that nobody is better than anyone else. We are not equal, either. We are all unique, and come bearing different gifts to this world. But we are all equal in intelligence. We might have different intellects (knowledge based on experience), but all have the same intelligence, which comes from a very sacred part of who you really are. We are from the same source. We are the source and, therefore, must own it and celebrate our privileged differences. Then you give the space for relationships to evolve, to emerge at their own pace and manner. Your relationships then release and bestow their own beauty.

Page 109

Unfortunately, most of us are psychologically driven. The choices we make translate into our present state of wellbeing. These states are transient in nature and, in the process, we get disheartened, lose trust, complain and start questioning those we love and those we rely upon.

I learnt to embrace my human nature, allowing the human in me, the beingness, to come alive and complete again. Jim Carrey, the comedian, remarks: "Once you realise, you're complete, then this life and everything in it becomes a form of play." We have all played games, and the outcome is always unpredictable.

And that is the fun of it, isn't it? Should our relationships be the same, letting them play out and seeing the beauty of each outcome? I say yes, and know experientially that we certainly should.

And even when relationships don't work out, can't we remind ourselves of these words the American composer and lyricist, Irving Berlin, wrote: "The song is ended... but the melody lingers on."?

I say yes, again, because such a relationship also had its own unique story and ending that brought you to this point in your life. Made you who you are. These relationships should be celebrated, and not leave a bitter taste in your mouth. Appreciate what you had, even for a short time, and think of the joy and happiness it brought you, even if for only a second. Just accept that the relationship was meant to happen, bring you its gift, and then go away. Stop being angry, vengeful and unhappy. Every relationship is taking you towards your own perfection.

Most of the time personality, not character, forms our identity. Instead of defining ourselves through the cultivation of virtue, we define and express ourselves through material possessions. Through conquest of the other (partner, children, colleagues). We give it the label "getting ahead". We develop moral values instead of virtues.

Morality is a personal set of values that is taught, typically, but not always, based upon a religion or a societal code of acceptable behaviour that is tied to consequences. Morality is subjective. Typically, with moral behaviour, there is a threat of punishment, negative outcomes or lack of respect if that behaviour or act is not pursued. What is equated as moral by one person or group, would not be seen as moral or just by another, or at a later point in time.

Virtue is a characteristic of our true, natural self. It is an expression of an intrinsic value that is not tied to a learned set of rules of society. To be virtuous is to be kind to others, not do harm and seek to find the best solutions for all parties, without concern for personal consequences, gain, or emotional benefit (the feel-good effect).

You can choose between self-improvement and self-sacrifice (which leads to self-realization). While self-improvement is essentially a solo act, i.e. usually picking up a book and learning the technique of improving the target area of your own personality, self-sacrifice on the other hand requires the willingness and the urge to learn and change your whole being – your character, from the Greek word, *kharakter*, meaning "engraved mark," "symbol or imprint on the soul." A character of compassion, love, forgiveness, sharing, non-judgement. Selfless. Such a character is grateful in every moment, no matter the outcome.

We can agree that self-centeredness and self-absorption are unappealing personality traits in a friend, colleague, or partner. We should learn to look at ourselves with the same critical eye. Both self-centred and self-absorbed people are more concerned with their image and materialistic things. They don't bother to take the time to understand another person's point of view or feelings. Do we maintain a sense of compassion and understanding towards others? Do we complain, whine all the time, no matter what? The fact that I had survived had convinced me that there was plan for me. I had to stop being needy, contracting and limiting myself.

I wanted to have the freedom to write my own story. To be the uncut block and the unbleached silk – that could be cut and sculptured as I wished. To be, as the Japanese aesthetics Furyu –just getting on with it and living with style, with rich poverty, and elegant simplicity.

As the Japanese aesthetic Yugen – in which the mystery of life is not a problem to be solved but a reality to be experienced. The deep mystery that is before all worlds is you, the unrecognised self and the authentic Awari, which is the regret of the passing of life which, somehow, makes that passing beautiful.

Bear your burden with courage and responsibility. When you're living in alignment with your true self, you develop a deep understanding and relationship with self. You're in alignment with your emotions, thoughts and beliefs. They begin to serve you, rather than work against you. You develop inner peace, harmony, joy and bliss.

You radiate passion, enthusiasm – those around you are drawn to you like a moth to a flame. Begin now. Take ownership of your life. Invest time and patience in getting to know you. And recognise your inner beauty. You'll attract the most amazing relationships (business, personal, professional, intimate, friendship), and create a life worthy of prosperity and abundance.

As I became more conscious of my own emotions, associated physiological and psychological sensations, and let go of things, emotions and events that didn't serve, I began to feel and enjoy the freedom that comes from letting go.

My realisation and acknowledgement of the uncomfortable-but-true habit of always wanting control constrained, restricted, stifled and suffocated me. It had kept me in fear, and I could not relax because I had to keep at it. I could not be spontaneous any more. You can imagine what this did to my relationships.

By freeing myself from these self-imagined and self-imposed burdens, I began to lose my sense of fear, and become more courageous and open to explore experiences and opportunities as they presented themselves. My relationships began to have more meaning and became more natural because now they arose from my heart and not my mind.

Instead of having hang-ups on universals, on huge abstracts and airy conceptions, I began to employ things that were very particular to who I really was.

In each moment of our lives, we make choices about how to relate and react to events and circumstances. You can either choose to succumb to bitterness, disillusionment, resentment and depression, or learn to forgive and heal yourselves. I now, after painful lessons, choose the latter.

You get anxious trying to describe and define your relationships. Allan Watts got it right – "Relationships are not a science - empirical constructs – that can be measured. It would be absurd to do so. The variables are infinite, and you have no idea what they are."

How many times have you picked up a magazine and answered twenty-five revealing relationship questions that can lead to better relationships? "Personal magic and profundity and not historical data make relationships work," remarks Alan Watts.

I learnt to be quiet and contemplative. Especially when it came to relationships, because relationships require subtlety - just like an artist who takes lots of information on board and turns it into an incredible picture.

I was the artist of my life, and I no longer wanted to make up a story of the future and spend all my time trying to make it come true, just because I did not want to be proven wrong. I wanted to live every moment of my life, and appreciated the opportunity to make mistakes, to fail, to experience pain and happiness. I wanted to be alive because of how I chose to face myself and the world. I wanted to live my life more consciously guided by whatever presented itself in the moment. To live fearlessly, regardless of the outcome. Not guided by an end-goal but by a deeper sense of self-awareness, knowing that I, too, was born with a unique gift to give to the world.

I didn't need to fit into any norm, any expectation, any sense of duty or commitment. This was liberating, and I found myself soaring in the skies once again. I could see and feel the world beneath me, and this gave me a sense of power, of knowing and feeling that everything had a place in existence. Instead of spending huge amounts of energy or effort in trying to hide or cover a part of my inherent character – the real me - I began to bring it out by expressing it. For example, I could now really express my emotions – empathy, sadness - when confronted by the suffering of others, and I am not trying to be benevolent – the smallest acts of kindness bring tears of happiness in me. A far cry from the cold-hearted person I had previously become. It wasn't all about me any more.

This is the key to individuality - taking everyday challenges as an opportunity to demonstrate who you are. By embracing every challenge and making it your own, you become fearless and develop your own narrative, moment by moment.

In this way, you begin to define yourself, not based on what is expected of you, but by who you are – who you were born to be. So, instead of looking for the ideal place or relationship, you simply become it. In short, you live it, because you love it. You learn to give, without condition, caveats or expectations. You connect to a stillness within you that is always free and happy.

Donald Walsh, the American author of the series *Conversations with God*, puts it in these words: "The most important message is that life is not about you. It has got nothing to do with you. It is to do with everybody's life you touch and the way you touch it. To discover yourself in the other. Be grateful all the time."

For the first time in my life, I understood how fear had kept me on a tightrope and from experiencing true love. Fear is the worst companion you can have. Fear influences behaviour, because it holds you back from doing things that you have the potential to do, and it makes you hesitate or hang back during social interactions for no good reason. Fear overrides our desires, holding us up, compromising what could have been a wonderful experience. Fear stops emotional growth and feelings. It keeps you feeling powerless and a victim. It stops you growing up and being responsible for yourself. It stops communication, trust and emotions. The challenge is to use love instead of fear in your life to move forward.

For true love to be experienced, our desire must be clear, strong and lasting. Without this, love cannot take shape. And when it does, time stands still. You become timeless. In such a moment, there is ecstasy, yet silence, unlimited joy, yet stillness, warmth, yet oblivion. It is experienced as "butterflies in the stomach", as fearlessness. Love is the purest expression of the universe, and requires no language for expression because it is felt the same way by the other. It is the universal language. It is expressed in music and literature. In poetry and prose.

Every relationship and experience, be it "good" or "bad", guides and grounds us to higher realisation and understanding. Kahlil Gibran, a Lebanese-American writer and poet, remarked, "I have learnt silence from the talkative, tolerance from the intolerant, kindness from the unkind, YET, I am ungrateful to them."

Yes, the whole universe is colluding to make us succeed in our pursuit of happiness.

I also realised that I had become used to the idea of suffering. Suffering had become the norm and, when there was nothing to worry about, I went searching for it. Or, worse still, created the circumstances for it, living on the edge, so to speak.

This becomes the story of our personal suffering. We become victims of this story. Instead, why not write your own story in your own way, by being the author, actor and witness of your own life?

In other words, your relationship with someone or something should not conflict with what you do within yourself. For example, when a relationship demands that you behave in a particular way, or has expectations that force you to, it becomes an obstacle leading to pain and suffering. In short, you should be realistic with yourself, and not concerned about making everything look calm and pretty.

Bad or failed relationships can lead to sadness, loneliness, low self-esteem and problems with health. Loneliness comes from not being with others, but also from not being with yourself. If you do not know yourself... you do not feel you are with somebody you know. A lonely existence.

Personal relationships can also fail because they are entered into through social pressures. For example, while falling in love is an important reason for getting married, social, family and peer pressures sometimes nudge you towards making personal decisions that you know are wrong and will eventually cause problems.

We all want to feel loved and satisfied in our relation- ships, and experience joy, happiness and fulfilment. We desire that all the people in our lives feel nurtured and loved. We may know intellectually that we are loved and cared for, yet feel emotionally unsatisfied. How do you articulate that? Here is a pointer by Henry David Throw, an American poet and philosopher: "You should aim to dwell as near as possible to the channel in which your life flows – it's about finding the people who are taking the same journey, connecting with people who feel as you do."

That is exactly what I did and discovered that, if you have the earnestness for freedom within you, you will find that power that we intuitively feel is with us. All you need to do is say "yes" to the moment, to surrender to the supreme authority within you. It takes an instant to realise this if your heart is ready, but we are too casual about it.

You cannot have peace externally if you don't have peace internally, and this requires faith and belief in yourself. I am reminded by these wise words of Rumi: "Oh my heart, don't become discouraged so easily. Have faith. In the hidden world, there are many mysteries, many wonders. Even if the whole planet threatens your life, don't let go of the Beloved's robe for even a breath."

Whether you believe in God or not, I think we all would, without a moment's hesitation, acknowledge that there is a place within us that we can draw upon in instances of great challenges, a sudden boost of power and resilience. All it requires is belief and faith in yourself. That moment, as brief as it might be, is so powerful that it will even surprise you. You might even say, "I didn't know I had it in me." You can call that whatever you wish, but it is there in each of us, whether we realise it or not. It takes only an instant to realise, or wake up to this. Each and every one of us needs to honour this place within us. It is where light, love, truth, peace and wisdom reside. It is difficult, and sometimes appears impossible, to wake up to that. We all have commitments, responsibilities and priorities - career, family, friends, children, travelling, health — that keep us busy under the label of "purpose".

We function through labels, but that identity is temporary, for that moment only. When we identify with them, we restrict our being, and it is full of anxiety and totally exhausting.

Anxiety arises from fear of the unknown. With the right guidance and practice, we can live in an undisturbed state of mind... the absence of mental conflict… the presence of serenity and tranquillity.

Before the heart attack, my rush to be "someone" was mainly because of spiritual ignorance. My message is simple - get rid of your spiritual ignorance and realise that you are much more than your thoughts and perceptions. You are the spirit, and it is your heart's desire and need to recognise this.

Karma and Samsara are an integral part the Guru ji's teachings. Karma simply means that every action has a consequence – "as he sows, so he reaps." Samsara is the cycle of reincarnation - those who come, must go in the end; they come and go, regretting and repenting. From every experience of suffering there is a lesson to learn. Suffering provides learning for spiritual growth. I attest to that.

We have, at some time or another, remembered and, if lucky, rediscovered a valuable or sentimental artefact that had been neglected and forgotten. My path to a joyous life was the rediscovery of the "misplaced, forgotten" self – the real me. For that to happen, I had to admit that my way had failed and that I needed to seek guidance from my Guru. He guided me to a clear recognition of what is here. I not only listened to his teachings, but practised them, too. This is a mortal body, and the game of life is to recognise itself, to its original self-knowing. To see the inner beauty of your heart.

Once that became clear, all the fears and doubts fell away. I began to see life as a blessing in every moment. I was no longer waiting to arrive at a projected state.

"Connect with your inner self… once you are truly at this infinite inner place, your true home, you will be at home anywhere, at any time, with anyone. A place where INFINITE possibility exists," remarks Angie Karan (poet and writer).

Yet we keep on making excuses to collect more and more information when we want to postpone a decision that we have already made, a while back, deep down in our hearts, that we intuitively know is right.

Make up your mind here and now and say, emphatically, "I am stopping making excuses for not meeting my true self. I have enough knowledge to know this, and will not waste time looking for more." Stop, recognise and acknowledge the inner beauty of your heart – the one-ness of everything.

That is Chapter 9.

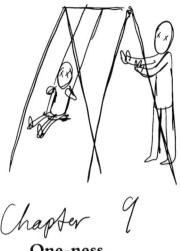

Chapter 9

One-ness

This chapter is about the realisation of the oneness of life, the discovery and experience of life as one continuous flow. The freedom and wisdom to choose what you need or desire, and the spontaneity that accompanies this freedom. It's like being the artist or musician in your relationships. Using feeling and deeper awareness to guide you, rather than over-relying on deconstructing everything in order to evaluate and measure different elements, when their value lies in the whole.

When in love, we don't see it as a relationship. It feels like as if we have collapsed into each other and there is a recognition of a shared being – a shared reality. We all long for this one-ness, just as we do when we get lost listening to music, or taking in a wonderful landscape or painting.

After my heart attack, I was touched by the kindness of friends and strangers, and began to recognise a sense of shared beingness and shared reality. My illness put me into a state of mind where I longed for the constant company of others.

This was strange, because previously, on most occasions, I longed to be alone, to be in my own company, make my own plans, and do as I pleased. After the heart attack, I developed a clear recognition that this mortal body had its limitations. It was William Blake (1757-1827) who said, "If the doors of perception were cleansed, everything would appear to man as it is – infinite."

Right from childhood, I have always been a person who, on a regular basis, attended the Sikh temple. The temple provided a place to socialise and engage in community projects, and offered spiritual guidance. Exactly in that order.

In my childhood, I always looked forward to meeting my friends and having the opportunity to play games that we mostly invented on the day. We also knew our parents would be busy preparing meals for the congregation and, just like us, have the chance to meet their own friends and catch up with the latest gossip and fashion trends.

We felt free and happy away from the constant gaze of our parents, mothers in particular, and this gave us a sense of adventure and independence. This sense of togetherness brought out the best in us. We couldn't wait until the next function.

With such a frame of mind, we also looked forward to an hour or so of spiritual teachings. We didn't feel forced to attend the temple. We went there with enthusiasm and genuine want. We always spoke in our mother tongue and, in hindsight, I believe we internalised our Punjabi culture.

When I was growing up in Kenya, our mum worked to take care of the house and our welfare, while our dad went out to work. Times are different now, and both parents juggle their time between work and looking after children and other family. That is the only way to cope with the increasing cost of living and, if I may dare say, our insatiable demand for things that fulfil the demands of our egos rather than their utility. Do we really need upgrades on everything? Perhaps I speak like an old man and not through the eyes of a young person.

We get dragged into new ways of living as our world changes, with fast-changing technologies and ways of thinking. I suppose we could say this for every generation. Change is inevitable, and they say you cannot stop progress. But it is difficult to cope with change.

Dan Millman, author of a series of books including *The Way of the Peaceful Warrior*, gives the following advice: "Now breathe and relax. Life comes to us as waves of change. We cannot predict or control those waves. But we can be better surfers.

"Practise and learn to be better surfers to manage the waves of change now and in each moment. Then the quality of the moment becomes the quality of our lives."

One of the ways that we seek to cope with change is to look for a structure to our lives so that we can feel a sense of control over our environment. Out of habit, we also look for structure in our relationships. But I have learnt that good relations cannot have a rigid structure. Relationships function best when left alone to emerge flexibly. Once you stop searching for a structure in relationships and just learn to feel the essence or substance of it, you discover that it's all one; it is homogeneous. It's akin to an artist or a musician, who flows with the feeling rather than sticking to a structure so tightly that it limits expression. Yes, there is a music sheet, a structure to the melody, but its interpretation is personal and fluid. That is what makes for an excellent conductor - the gift of bringing everything together in a way that is beyond the individual notes of the different musical instruments.

He can merely feel and the notes and create something more than their sum total. I think that was the experience we had when we went to the temple when growing up. Individual people, separate actions – all creating an experience that was comforting, exciting, enriching and uplifting, and all of these at the same time.

There was a natural flow of life. In comparison, modern times seem to be about clinical efficiency. Alan Watts makes a valid observation about how we see life. He comments, "It seems society has turned into an empirical scientist, who deconstructs everything so that it can be measured. There are too many variables in relations, which one would you measure? It's about being truthful to yourself and honest in your relation-ships and not clinical."

It is also true that we lose our spontaneity as we get older. And this is mainly because it is killed within us through culturalization – the process of teaching values and norms appropriate or necessary in that culture and world view. For example, children are given a pat on the back when parents feel they have done well, and are criticised when they don't. In this way, spontaneity is killed. They are taught to follow rules. Maybe they should also be encouraged to play more, to balance their development. Learning through play is a well-established and central principle of personal development.

The long and short of it is that, when we become self-conscious of what we are doing, we lose a very beautiful part of us. All because we must observe societal rules and, in the process, develop self-consciousness which, although it is a great thing to have, restricts us in many ways.

For example, self-consciousness gives rise to a roller-coaster of emotions because we are – consciously or unconsciously – carrying out actions that are designed to reduce uncertainty, failure and personal pain.

There are too many variables in human behaviour, and it is literally impossible to predict anything with certainty. I know now, in hindsight, that it's impossible to predict a pathway to a relationship - personal or otherwise. This realisation is liberating. It has freed me from the constant thinking and planning that went into everything I did. I realise that, in the process of making myself safe by having rules and protocol of my design, I had in fact trapped myself in a stressful life that eventually led to a heart attack.

I have now experienced first-hand how it feels not to be bottled up, to be spontaneous, to feel part of something bigger than me and just flow with whatever is happening in the moment. This is oneness - going with the natural flow. There is a certain discipline required for this, but it requires being spontaneous, too.

There is no technique to having a healthy relationship. The secret lies in the realisation that the more you try to plan an outcome, the more obstacles you create for yourself. Planning a relationship implies a personal agenda. Imagine what would happen if you said, "I will show you my agenda if you show me yours," when you want to build a relationship with someone. So why is it that we hold our agendas so close to the chest? Because we all want to maintain a certain level of control for our current and future circumstances.

Furthermore, you cannot realise your relationship's fullest potential, because personal agendas are constantly changing. These kinds of relationship are difficult, because they are based on trade-offs. And when an agenda surfaces at some point in the relationship, the consequences can be devastating.

Unfortunately, the focus then becomes how to "fix" the other. To change the "other" whilst the "other" is doing the same. It is difficult to admit this and, eventually, the sparks taper off. We blame the "other", and the ability to rationalise keeps us safe.

On the other hand, if you go into a relationship without preconceived "planning", with no expectations or a particular desired outcome, and be true to yourself, with honesty and openness and respecting yourself as well as the other - see what happens and where it leads. Not reacting, but responding as the relationship develops. Being flexible, letting go and being open to new things can only bring you closer together. Open-mindedness is a characteristic that involves being receptive to a wide variety of ideas, arguments and information.

Being open-minded is generally considered a positive quality. It is a necessary ability in order to think critically and rationally. Please note that I am not using the term "open-minded" as a synonym for being non-prejudiced or tolerant. The opposite of open-minded is closed-minded, or dogmatic. People who are more closed-minded are usually only willing to consider their own viewpoints, are not receptive to other ideas and usually have their own agenda. When you are not open-minded, and things begin to go sour, you usually act out of emotions such as anger or despair; in extreme cases, physical violence towards others or self-harm may result.

As a first step, I had to admit to this weakness within myself. My recent, more careful, study of the spiritual dimensions of our lives had taught me that events, emotions and moods happen, come and go. I learnt to separate myself from these tides. This was made easier because I no longer looked more for my own clarity and comfort about what I was doing, rather than for acceptance from others.

Page 127

As time went by, I began to feel a sense of commitment and contentment in relationships. I felt at ease, something that I had not felt for a long, long time. How could this be possible when there was no effort on my part?

It took me a while to grasp that life could continue in amazing ways without me constantly thinking about it. From the love and care that I received, I slowly developed a natural trust and recognition that what was needed was being provided for me as it was required in that moment.

Don't get me wrong. I am not advocating becoming a bum, although that must have some positives, too. The essence of what I am saying is that, as I continued to carry on with my endeavours in life after my heart attack, everything just fell effortlessly into place. All this was done with a very different mindset - surrendering to life and what it brought up – learning and knowing that life is whatever it needs to be, not judging any more - and many different doors began to open for me. This is what I meant by being content. The Sikh Gurus call this *sehaj vasta* (deep contentment).

Idris Shah, also known by the pen-name Arkon Daraul, an author and teacher in the Sufi tradition who wrote over three dozen books, said, "Enlightenment must come little by little, otherwise it would overwhelm." You must be willing and patient.

Knowing something experiential is different from something that you are told by someone else, or have read about. But this is extremely difficult, because we find it difficult to let go of our perceptions, habits and the narratives we tell ourselves. This keeps us locked up in a perpetual cycle of struggles. We are never free from this.

You must have an earnestness, a hunger within you for this freedom. You just need to say, "Yes, I am ready to be guided from the innermost place part of myself." We are intuitive beings but somehow, in our conditioning (attachment to shifting identities), we have been trained to rely on process thinking, trying to figure things out and treating life as if it were a strategy.

Instead, be clear to your true nature, the beauty of your inner self. Try to find that space within you that is unchanging. And, with that, comes the acceptance of the "what is" in every moment, which means living without the sense of the need to control. No control means there is no conflict, as conflict is a result of thought that relies on personal agendas. I pray and try to use guidance from my Gurus for the courage to trust and let go. Henri Nouwen (1932-1996), a Dutch Catholic priest, professor, writer and theologian, puts it in these simple words: "To pray is to listen to the One who calls you 'my beloved daughter,' 'my beloved son,' 'my beloved child.' To pray is to let that voice speak to the centre of your being, to your guts, and let that voice resound in your whole being."

The urge to always be in control leads you down a path of suffering, because you are attempting to put "brakes" on life, to straighten it, but you only end up digging a deeper hole. The "brakes" come in the form of critical thought about your own personal agenda of seeking happiness and power through attachment to a particular idea, projected by your thoughts or mind. You have to learn the art of letting go.

Page 129

The Sikh Gurus give a simple message – the destination of our journey in the human form is to achieve a blissful state *(anand)* and be in harmony with all creation. To achieve this, they advocate the practice of compassion, service to others, forgiveness, contentment and unconditional love for all creation. It is the stepping-stone to finding the inner unchanging part of yourself. Your spirit.

We can learn a lot from children, who have an innocence that lets them enjoy every experience in their lives. They don't make judgements, or hold grudges for long. They are fluid in their responses, accepting everything that comes their way with wonder and a sense of adventure. And, very importantly, they are spontaneous in their reactions.

We know we are at ease, happy and at our best when there is no pretending, and this opens up possibilities. Guided by what is meaningful, your true natural guidance emerges within you. You must have faith in the real you.

"You cannot be who you are not," says Ana Claudia Antunes, in *Dancing as One (The DAO) Workbook Illustrated*, "simply rest, sit still and unknot. You may even try to emulate and inspire, but it's the inner self that you'll transpire."

But this is no easy task, and Musashi Miyomoto, (*A Book of Five Rings: The Classic Guide to Strategy*) provides this wonderful advice: "Even if you strive diligently on your chosen path day after day, if your heart is not in accord with it, then even if you think you are on a good path, from the point of view of the straight and true, this is not a genuine path. If you do not pursue a genuine path to its consummation, then a little bit of crookedness in the mind will later turn into a major warp. Reflect on this."

I suppose one way to know that you are on the right path is to examine your intentions and actions. When intentions are different from actions, our mind gets busy inventing stories to avoid getting caught out. This is very tiring, as continued efforts are required to justify these actions. No matter how hard one tries, gradually the true intentions surface. The result is misery.

And when actions reflect our true intentions, we live without fear, stand up tall, take responsibility and accept any outcome, happy in the knowledge that we did our best and that, next time, we will do even better.

I believe we should remind ourselves that actions must come from true intentions. In this way, we can open the gates to our deeper inner self which, in turn, then guides us to happiness. We begin to believe in ourselves and shed the clouds of doubt.

Doubts lead to confusion and uncertainty. Being unsure brings up all sorts of negative feelings, such as uneasiness, unhappiness and confusion. By connecting to our inner self, we become steadfast and feel safer in our inner sanctuary – a state of mind that intuitively knows that we, all of us, have an infinite capacity for love, forgiveness and compassion. In this space, you have the ability to consciously choose your emotional state.

You feel relaxed and at ease in your grounded inner state. There is a certain calmness and un-rushed feeling to it. When I say relaxed, it's not what we usually refer to, a process of relaxing e.g. "I am going to relax with this book" – certainly not. What I refer to as the relaxed state is a chosen attitude that arises from the under-standing that, as spiritual beings, we possess the ability to choose our dominant emotional states.

We all have a past and have made mistakes and guilt weighs us down. Mistakes can be intentional or unintentional because the motives seemed right at the time. At times we hurt others to make ourselves look better, take advantage of others to get ahead, treat others with disdain and disgust because we feel we are better than them and somehow entitled to do so.

We have all become experts in justifying, rational-ising and having our way. My heart attack was a direct result of this. Years of stress directly related to making the wrong choices that I knew were not perfect, and rationalised as necessary for future security. If anything, the stark message that this near-death experience gave me was to learn to pause and evaluate, and admit to and drop the dead weight.

It's only then that you can take the next steps to happiness. In my case, I knew I could not do this on my own and needed guidance from my Guru. He offered me a way to get out of this self-constructed trap. He showed me how to use the power of earnest prayer to lead a meaningful life.

Instead of leading a meaningful life, we continue to be creatures of habit and routine. As soon as we open our eyes in the morning, we have a list of things to do. There is a sequence to our day, and every minute is booked. We end the day by making another to-do list.

We are intuitively curious and want to feel, grasp, explore and understand every experience we have. And that is wonderful, because we are a part of the universe created for the experience of all. But, somewhere in our lives, we lose ourselves in the mêlée that we create for ourselves. Our attention wanders all the time and we miss, overlook, or ignore the beauty of what we are experiencing in the moment. We lose sight of the temporary nature of all things. I think we can all agree that everything we see and do is temporary, fluid and has a time limit.

We also get so caught up in the roles we play that we start manipulating others to suit our desires. This only leads to temporary happiness, until the next "fix". What you sow is what you reap. Give love and you get love back, be compassionate and feel it coming back, give hate and hate comes back.

Shams Tabrizi, Rumi's teacher, puts it this way – "This world is like a mountain. Your echo depends on you. If you scream good things, the world will give it back. If you scream bad things, the world will give it back. Even if someone says badly about you, speak well about him. Change your heart to change the world."

So why not accept these rules and experience life by experiencing your oneness? Underpin your intention with love, and drive your actions with compassion, understanding, patience, empathy and forgiveness. Place your faith in the hands of this universal one-ness and accept every experience as it is, with grace and thanks. The psychologist, Carl Jung, remarks, "We cannot change anything until we accept it. Condemnation does not liberate, it oppresses." The point is that your happiness lies in reframing events to accept what is, and letting go of what you cannot control. It seems difficult, but it really isn't – you begin by slowing down and finding time for contemplation.

Page 133

We rush around and get to the point where we don't even have a moment to pause and reflect on the direction we are going, and give too much importance to what is happening outside us. We often say that we are good people because we do good things, such as donating to the needy and helping those that need assistance.

Look deeper and you find these actions are carried out to make you feel good about yourself, so that you can continue your life as it is. You expect to be rewarded in return for your "good" acts – it is a transaction – I did this good act and expect to get rewarded in some way.

From the moment we wake up to the time we fall asleep (in dreams, too) we play many roles – father, mother, son, daughter, husband, wife, boss, team captain, teacher, learner and so on. This is wonderful, as they provide us with ways and opportunities to have different experiences.

But, when we confuse role-playing with identity, or our one-ness, we develop "tunnel vision" in our daily lives, especially when we are busy, stressed and tired. In such moments, remind yourself of your one-ness.

Use your eyes to look at Mother Earth, that keeps giving, never complaining. Taste the water that nourishes your thirst, never judging you. Feel the constant, uninterrupted air that provides you with life, never complaining.

Learn from the plants and the trees, which accept rain and sunshine whenever provided, never demanding, always patient, always in one place. Listen to the constant music being played by all of them, always humming, never stopping, and always thankful.

Honing your mind and practising meditation, daily, can help you become more focused, empathetic and aware. Training your brain in this way can open you up to a better understanding of how your mind works and how to enjoy the present moment.

Meditation, or mindfulness, is a way of cutting out the "noise" from our lives and recognising that perceptions are just thoughts that have no power over you. You are more than your thoughts.

We are always on the move, consciously or out of habit. Always thinking about what we must do next, or achieve next. It gives us a sense of control, and we like to be in charge and give our actions labels, like success, high achiever, responsible family man, go-getter, and so on.

But there is no end to our wanting, and we get more and more burdened as we demand more out of ourselves. But we are limited in what we can do and, eventually, with time, get broken. My recent experience is that, while it is great to aspire to great things in your life, don't try to figure everything out and treat life as a strategy.

Instead, rein in your inner self by using your senses of perception - tongue not to slander, eyes not to look at your neighbour's yard, ears not for listening to gossip. Retune yourself and be in harmony with all you touch. Write your own tune, be the orchestra, the conductor and the listener. Be the one-ness.

In this way, you can use your mind for practical things. It has become deeply ingrained in our psyche that to achieve anything, including love, requires an action, an effort. If we can learn to surrender to the moment, we can experience pure joy and embrace our one-ness.

Travelling is fun and exciting when we are with like-minded friends and family. And I think this is an important point to make. As I recovered from my heart attack, I was introduced to a lot of support groups who had gone through similar experiences.

It really felt great to know that others had gone through the same pain, survived and led full lives. On reflection, it's quite bizarre how the pain and experiences of others helps us cope with our own pain. I suspect it is the feeling of one-ness that underpins this. You feel part of the same club.

While I recovered, I also began to attend the Sikh temple on a daily basis. In the company of others (the *sadh sangat*), I had begun a process of self-inquiry, and the shared space and energy with the *sangat* had a huge, positive impact on my recovery. In the Siri Guru Granth Sahib (818:6) it says, "Joining the Saadh Sangat, the Company of the Holy, I have found peace and tranquillity; I shall not wander away from there again." In the presence of my loved ones, the support groups and the temple community, I intuitively felt comfort, in the knowledge that my needs - mental, physical and spiritual - would somehow be met as they arose.

It took some time and effort, but I could now finally get glimpses of a version of myself which was better than the various limited identities of myself I had formed. That felt wonderfully empowering and powerful.

It's not something that you can hold on to, and is purely experiential. In moments that I experience this, there is a stark realisation that this is all that exists — the one-ness. The company of the *sadh sangat* infuses me gently with love in my quest for one-ness, and rocks me gently in the comfort of the lap of my Guru.

Beyond the *sadh sangat*, the realisation finally dawned on me that we all exist within *sangat*. We do not live in isolation. I feel *sangat* is with me daily along my journey, and in whoever crosses my path from moment to moment.

I now acknowledge, experientially, that a single energy force — the one-ness- exists within all of creation. Every moment of my life is the culmination of not only all my efforts and hard work, but also the efforts of many souls, and incidents, that have touched, and continue to touch, my path.

I enjoy and embrace the discovery of that interconnectedness, and live in the deep knowledge that I am surrounded by unconditional love and being guided by an intelligence that knows my every need and dream.

"The universe is a complete unique entity," remarks Shams Tabrizi. "Everything and everyone are bound together with some invisible strings. Do not break anyone's heart; do not look down on weaker than you. One's sorrow at the other side of the world can make the entire world suffer; one's happiness can make the entire world smile."

Simple yet powerful words to live by. You just need to have the hunger for it.

We seek the support of others when in the quest for something that is beyond our understanding and grasp. This is especially true when seeking spiritual guidance. No one exists in a vacuum, and sangat is critical to self-development.

Page 137

My Guru provided me with this support, alerting me to the many pitfalls on the journey, guiding me gently, through practical practices, to turn my heavily-laden ship of life. You have to put the guidance into practice, otherwise you are only gathering knowledge. Praxis is the process by which a lesson or skill is enacted, embodied, or realized. "Praxis" may also refer to the act of engaging, applying, exercising, realizing, or practising ideas. The Sikh does this through *simran* (application of Guru's teachings in everyday life) and *sewa* (service to others). I had to, and did, with my Guru as guide and protector.

"The true teacher defends his pupils against his own personal influence," says Amos Bronson Alcott (an American teacher, philosopher and reformer). He continues, "He inspires self-trust. He guides their eyes from himself to the spirit that quickens him. He will have no disciples." My Guru was all this, and much more. He is my breath, sustainer and protector.

Intentions drive our actions in everyday life, while spiritual intention is driven by an unquestioned motivation to expand yourself beyond your everyday, personal life (family, work, ambition).Clarifying and focusing on your own true reason for "being-ness, or one-ness" is one of the simplest, yet most profound, ways to cut through a lot of fragmented truths. Your focused spiritual intent, when made conscious, gives you a way to emulate your greater self, moment by moment.

This I do through conscious living, by practising the qualities of my higher self (compassion, selfless service, forgiveness), which gently mould me into my one-ness. It begins with a specific activity, such as helping at a charity event, or a simple act of kindness, but later becomes a way of life.

We have all fallen in love. Love gives us a sense of happiness in the other person's joy. But how do we love ourselves – the one-ness in us, our heart, soul and mind? When in love, we bask in a warm glow, and no challenge seems impossible. We are driven by love, and our whole life revolves around love. Love is what gives our life meaning. Love is more than just a feeling, and it draws us toward one another and joins us together. Love is at the core of our very existence.

Pause and consider this. Don't we think in terms of a set of trained responses, or instinctual patterns, as if on autopilot? Do we know what or why we are doing the things we do most of the time? Don't we come up with reasons such as "It's who I am," to explain why we do what we do? Perhaps it's an avoidance mechanism that is borne out of fear.

"When your life is filled with the desire to see the holiness in everyday life, something magical happens. Ordinary life becomes extraordinary, and the very process of life begins to nourish your soul," remarks Rabbi Harold Kushner.

We determine our worthiness, our path, our rewards, our pain and our end destination. We should not sell ourselves short and limit ourselves through our limited pre-judgments, assumptions, feelings and comfort zones.

We might be inclined to uncover identity through the family tree, try to be defined by a specific, uniquely personal characteristic, or, perhaps, pick a particular trait to describe ourselves. We still feel incomplete, lost, fleetingly happy and briefly content.

Page 139

In our journey of life, we develop certain habits, opinions and mindsets and, when we don't get what we want, we get disappointed; there is always someone else to blame. But, once we experience our one-ness, we intuitively realise that there is a deeper, universal order that is running the "show" of life. Others might call this spiritual acceptance.

When things are not going our way, and especially when events have already transpired and cannot be changed, can we let go of the idea that things should go our way? When we resist, we hand over the power of our emotional wellbeing to that situation - to other people or events.

Acceptance is the willingness to let go of our emotional opposition to what is happening in the moment. Accepting the "what is", without judgement. It means "It is". Even though we can't see it, or understand why it's happening now, we should just let go and let our one-ness take over. This is the foundation of humility, and the path to contentment.

At some point in our lives, we come to a realisation that there is more to living than what we continue to seek through our daily deliberations. We begin to feel imprisoned, suffocated, and desperate to find a way out. We follow, with diligence, our dreams and our aspirations. There is no stopping as we move from one achievement (or failure) to the next and the next. That is how life works, we think. But, at some point, we become so entangled in the cage we create around ourselves, that we seek release and assistance.

I am reminded of Bob Marley – we've got to fulfil the book - *Redemption Song* – "Emancipate yourselves from mental slavery; None but ourselves can free our minds. Have no fear for atomic energy, Cause none of them can stop the time. How long shall they kill our prophets, while we stand aside and look? Ooh! Some say it's just a part of it."

The is the first step to emancipation, for liberation. With time, our faith builds up in our one-ness and we begin to receive unexpected gifts and a sense of deep contentment.

Knowledge is not wisdom. We rationalise our short-comings by making others look worse than us. We do this by telling ourselves stories of sometimes dubious merit, to justify our behaviour. We find comfort in this.

It makes us feel important, wise, knowledgeable. It makes us feel great.

The path of spiritual development comes from the deepest level of our beings. It is the very same drive that expresses itself in a child's curiosity or in the sprouting of a seed. Seek that, be the child, be the seed, innocent, letting things come to it, never chasing, never challenging, no expectations, always knowing (not knowledge) that what is needed will be provided.

We feel anxious because of fear — of failure, of change, of financial security, of losing love, of one's safety. We feel like this because we don't have control over every eventuality. We call it risk and uncertainty.

Human nature is blind to problems in our character. We are good at observing the mistakes and short-comings of others, but not our own. We have become like the person who looks in the mirror, sees the faults and then walks away, doing nothing about them.

Page 141

We all have expectations - career, love, family, status, house, friends, power and, rightly, work hard to achieve them. We also try to live up to the expectations of others. It is tiring. In the process, we build walls around us that hide the real essence of who we are, and the hole we dig gets bigger and the cage stronger. "How hurtful it can be to deny one's true self," says June Ahern (self-published author) "and live a life of lies just to appease others."

Pause and think. If we justify our faults, we may as well not bother to look for them. Be willing to admit when wrong and then take the next step forward. Seek your one-ness.

Learn to get in touch with the silence within yourselves and know that everything in this life has a purpose. "There are no mistakes, no coincidences. All events are blessings given to us to learn from," remarks Elizabeth Kübler-Ross, the Swiss-American psychiatrist, a pioneer in near-death studies and the author of the ground-breaking book *On Death and Dying*. Taking credit for something allows us to believe in ourselves, in our capabilities, in our invincibility - whether true or false. Who hasn't had the experience of asking something higher than us for help, of opening possibilities? When insights are provided, a solution or guidance, we take personal credit for it. Suddenly, we are the genius and we lose the connection to that which brought us the insight in the first place. Why not constantly maintain the connection to our inner space through regular meditation, and be rid of this separation from our natural expression?

Step into the direction of "one-ness", and move out from something-ness into full-ness. Be patient, trusting that everything is connected, that each experience takes you towards your full-ness. Imagine endless peace, harmony, and unconditional love. Imagine no fear, and equality in all things. This is One-ness. You still have a mind, but you are no longer caught in it; no longer identified with it. Aspire to be better than the best you can – and the whole universe will work with you.

Quantum physics talks about a unified field, which underlies and connects everything in creation. Who we are is pure consciousness, or One-ness, expressing itself in different forms at different times in our evolution. Pure Consciousness, which is eternal and timeless, is the

One-ness; we are the separation or the duality.

We can have direct experience of One-ness through meditation. When we slip into the spaces between our thoughts, we become One-ness. One-ness isn't just experiencing something; it's a state of being. We've all had random, unexpected glimpses of One-ness. Perhaps you were watching a beautiful sunset and had that moment when you felt like you merged with the whole of creation; or when you madly fell in love and the bottom of your heart fell out.

"In one-ness, love is patient and kind. It does not envy or boast, it is neither proud nor rude. It is not self-seeking, easily angered, and does not keep a record of wrongs. Love does not delight in evil, but rejoices with the truth. It always hopes, always perseveres." (I Corinthians 13:4-8a ESV)

We all long for a state of happiness and peace, and make preparations to achieve these – getting more qualifications, enhancing performance, making the right connections. Eventually, we get so involved in our daily struggles and the need to get ahead that we feel disconnected from who we are.

No matter how much we understand, or don't, about our life, we still must do the living. Our struggles determine our successes. Sometimes we find life a burden. Life becomes a routine, a pattern. Sometimes life is a joy. We get restless, disheartened, unhappy, and it becomes important to get back to our one-ness and be complete. To anchor in a permanent state of pure intelligence, which is our true essence. This is achieved through constant meditation and the practice of compassion, forgiveness and selfless service in the company of those who are on the same path. This raises us above transient experiences and into a space of contentment and bliss. Stay put and experience all the emotions of living, of being-ness. Anchored, like a ship, not changing its character no matter the storm, the calm. Just riding the waves of life and experiencing whatever may come our way.

It is easy to become confused, lose focus and believe what comes to mind superficially, rather than what has been learned about what is true. Our living can be more purposeful, have constancy of purpose and a truth that is not swayed by circumstances or our external fallibilities when we make decisions anchored in our one-ness. Our one-ness lets us see the light of love within and obtain clarity in our lives. And then we accept the outcome of every decision, because it came from a place of truth and love within us. We lose anxiety and confusion, knowing that this one-ness has brought us far, is devoted to us and is never going to stop loving.

The Sikh Gurus guided me to search within myself to find my own answers and meanings. Importantly, they taught me to recognize that we are all different, all unique and beautiful, with different dreams, aspirations and talents. Dr Helena Cronin, a British Darwinian philosopher and rationalist, calls it "Privileged difference."

We're conditioned to equate love with longing. We often hear the proverb "Absence makes the heart grow fonder." Our longing builds in direct proportion to the "other's" longing. We waste our lives in a state of longing and search. Restless, unsure and fearful that we may not find that special one.

It is sad that the only time we feel in love and certain is when the "other" isn't fully available. Why not let yourself be with someone who's fully available, and there's no longing? Let that someone be your one-ness, that is never uncertain and fearful of finding love.

We all make mistakes. If we were afraid of making them, we would not be creative. Learning from our mistakes is the important thing, and we improve and get better with experience. Some mistakes are avoidable, but we get carried away in the moment. Experience hasn't taught us. That is how life works. Until we finally give in, and surrender to experience. We blame ourselves and others for time wasted, and end up living in guilt.

We should invest in rediscovering our one-ness, from which arise ideas, creativity, resilience, openness, forgiveness and fearlessness. And, through this, we become ageless learners and build our own unique framework of life. Practising through actions, and not words, to become experiential learners.

You might have heard the story about the jar of life - stones, pebbles and sand. An old professor filled an empty jar with large stones. Everybody said the jar was full. No, said the professor, and brought out the pebbles and sand. What can we learn from this? The important lesson is that, if we don't put all the larger stones in the jar first, we will never be able to fit all of them in later. Sadly, we give priority to the smaller things in life (pebbles & sand). Our lives get filled up with less important things, leaving little or no time for the things in our lives that are most important to us. What are the large stones in your life? Wealth, family, friends, love, health...? You need just one big stone in your jar of life.

A stone that has, within it, all the other stones, pebbles and sand of your life. You don't have to seek outside for this magical stone. It has already been placed in your jar. Give priority to finding this within you. If you don't, you will miss out on life altogether.

"There is nothing outside of yourself that can ever enable you to get better, stronger, richer, quicker, or smarter," says Miyamoto Musashi, in *The Book of Five Rings*. "Everything is within. Everything exists. Seek nothing outside of yourself."

If we valued simplicity, our lives would become fuller because we would recognise that there is a natural order to everything. There is a divine order, and it determines the rhythm of life. Look at nature. The plants and animals know this. Let us make our lives simpler by recognising there is an order to all existence, and stop using our cunning to outsmart the natural order of the universe. We can seek the company of those who have recognised and surrendered to the rhythm of life. They will help us to re-connect with our own inner source of wisdom. There has always been a plan for us, and we need not get side-tracked by busy-ness.

When you find the love of your life (and it may even be one-sided), what is the condition of your mind, your heart? Where do all the praises we sing for the "one" arise from? Aren't they rooted in a deeper place within you that cannot be pin-pointed? Doesn't this love come within a deep place that feels lost without the "one"? Feel incomplete? When this happens, the only way we remember the "one" is through constant praise. We cannot stop repeating, "I love this, and I love that about you." We are eager to share this praise with others, too.

We want to share every moment and experience with the special one. These praises are not reasoned out. Nor justified by some thinking process. They just are. They are your bare self, stripped of every pretence, world view.

We need to get to know ourselves. Our companion is within us, and it is only us who have chosen to ignore him. A companion that has humility, never judging, always forgiving and compassionate. Always there, with you and for you.

"The first piece, which is the most important, is that which comes within the souls of people when they realize their relationship, their one-ness with the Universe and all its powers and when they realize that at the centre of the Universe dwells the Great Spirit and that this centre is really everywhere, it is within each of us" says Black Elk, an Oglala Sioux.

Page 147

We live according to the habits we have formed, patterns established, moods we experience. "That is the way I am," we say. Others do, too. That is how they know you. It is how you know yourself. And we use words like "it's OK", "it is a passing phase," "tolerate me," "it will pass."

"Oh, what a tangled web we weave, when first we practise to deceive," is a famous quote in the poem *Marmion*, written by the Scottish author and novelist, Sir Walter Scott. The poem describes the lengths that Lord Marmion and his mistress, a nun, go to in plotting to entrap a woman he lusts for. In the end, Marmion and the nun fall foul of their own web of lies. The nun is bricked-up alive and Marmion dies dishonourably on the battlefield.

Each of us is busy building our own web of lies. Driven by a blinding rush to get ahead of the pack, no matter who gets crushed on the way. Entrapping and suffocating our own lives, slowly but surely. Getting bricked-up alive. What will this bring but dishonour? We can consciously choose another way of living.

To live a life built on hard and honest work, compassion, selflessness, contentment and wisdom. To live in the embrace of your one-ness, that protects and guides you to be creative, adventurous and fearless. Never plotting for the downfall of others, but seeking the wellbeing of all.

"A man's character is his fate," remarks the Greek philosopher Heraclitus (540BC-480BC).

Throughout our lives we accumulate experiences. Our perception of ourselves is dependent on our experiences. And there are times, especially as we get older - more experienced – when we begin to walk with stooped shoulders. We get overburdened. Sometimes reaching breaking-point. We label these as psychological in nature, and seek interventions accordingly. To drill down into the psychological mind to seek out the source of our suffering and unhappiness.

No matter the burden you carry, it is never too late to come to reconnect with your one-ness. My Guru did this, and he did not even judge me. There was one condition, and that was to put into practice – praxis - the teachings of the Guru. Just listening, or going to the temple was not quite enough. The word "praxis" comes, via the medieval Latin, from Greek - doing, action, from "prassein - to do", practice (Merriam-Webster).

Meditating and self-less service of others is the praxis of the teachings of the Guru. It begins with total trust in your teacher and guide. I understood for the first time the power of prayer, and what it really meant to be in the Guru's grace.

It meant being grateful for every breath I took and gradually, as the heavy burden of a life not well-lived dropped off my shoulders, I began to live life in a way that I had forgotten to live.

We are either being judged by others or, worse still, our own selves. It is constant and never lets up. Measuring our worth against each judgement, living in fear and behaving and acting to please others. Or, alternatively, we are very busy trying to maintain the status quo.

Page 149

Whose life are we living? Whose judgement do we value the most, and why? Living becomes a serious task and taxing.

This is how we get caught in psychological traps of the mind. No matter the condition of our physical, mental or financial wellbeing, we can seek guidance to reconnect to our one-ness. A guide that never holds a grudge, wipes our slate clean, lightens our load and infuse us with new breath of life.

A life of renewed vigour and freshness, without fear and full of love. To live a life of contentment whilst seeking your highest dreams and aspirations. But with a difference now; no longer swimming against the current, but with the current of life.

Experiencing joy in each moment. Accepting the outcome of each action with grace, knowing that your one-ness is working on your behalf, ensuring an outcome that does not bring suffering and judgement.

There is an unexplained mad rush to achieve goals, successes, get somewhere, or find love. Behind this rush is desperation. What if we don't make it? What if we do, and realise that it wasn't what we wanted? Do we, can we, start all over again? How do I hold on to my achievements? In the end, we sell ourselves short and settle for much less that what we are capable of.

We cling to life. The choices we make translate into habits and patterns, and anything that does not fit within these feels unsafe and uncertain. We unwittingly end up constraining ourselves and limiting the possibilities that come from a limited capacity to think and act outside the box.

We also carry out a constant internal dialogue which keeps us rational, or so we think. "I don't have a choice, I have responsibilities," we rationalise, and "At least it pays the bills," we say. But at what personal cost and sacrifice? A heart attack?

As I have discovered, there is another way to live. It requires the breaking of these habits and patterns of thinking, and waking up to a greater reality that has serendipity at its very foundation.

We are searching for answers to everything, and search in all sorts of sources to obtain them. We then make an informed decision. But, when things don't go our way, we question the reliability and validity of the information and, when we do get it right, we keep on repeating the same actions, expecting the same result.

We treat life as a chemical reaction. When you mix chemicals in a certain way, you expect the same result. But life is not like that, is it? We never get the perfect answer that works all the time. So, where do we search for the right answers? Who can we trust to provide them?

I knew of only one place, a place that I had known all my life but largely ignored – the Sikh Gurus. *Kerr-nae* is a Punjabi word meaning crying out aloud for the beloved. It is a word usually used to describe the cry of loss, emptiness and sadness when somebody close dies. To cry in pain for that which cannot be replaced. It is not reciprocal, as the other is gone. It is love based on fear of loss and the loss of comforts the other brought you. Eventually, we move on and life goes on, remembering the loss occasionally with a fond smile or thought.

I have survived for over two decades after my heart attack. If events had gone the other way I, too, would have become a distant memory. A sobering thought, and something that I ponder about often.

The expression "no pain, no gain" can be attributed to physical and mental wellbeing. But, when it comes to spiritual wellbeing, it is faith that counts. No matter how much penance you pay, physical endurance you undertake, knowledge you gather, visits you make to holy places, charity work you do, or pilgrimages you make, if faith is missing, you have wasted your efforts.

Faith is nothing but having the belief that the world borrows its existence from you. An acceptance that each moment of your life is as it should be. Not questioning, but saying "Yes, it is as it should be." When you are flying thousands of feet in the air, you trust the pilot, the crew and the plane that you will get there.

Because we have faith, no questions arise. Faith means to be fearless and trust in one-ness. Faith means not even knowing your journey or your destination.

Faith is about "being" and not about "becoming". "Being" implies acceptance of yourself as the spirit with virtues such as compassion, forgiveness and service to others. "Becoming", on the other hand, implies a process towards some vision or goal. You cannot "become" what you already are.

Our quest for love is at the core of everything we do. We use various ways to impress the other and capture the attention of the other. We endeavour to show our best side and hide or mask the not-so-good. In short, we pretend to be someone we are not and, at the same time, the other is also busy playing the same game.

In short, we are always busy trying to get noticed and impress. Eventually, reality sets in and the honeymoon is over, simply because we cannot continue to pretend all the time. It is hard work being someone we are not, and we crave for our own "freedom" and "space".

So how can we find true love and love effortlessly? It is by being the real us. All we need to get noticed is to acknowledge our one-ness, and then love becomes effortless. All our other loves come to us. Such a simple secret, because our Valentine is within us.

When we share our lives with somebody who understands us well, life becomes joyous and inspiring. It then doesn't matter what we share or what we have. The act of sharing even the simplest experience becomes the focus of our being. We feel loved, worthwhile and centred.

We long to find such a companion who understands us well. It is not easy to be alone, because it gets lonely and we feel lost, without an anchor. We ask for advice and direction from other people who have found love and happiness. We, too, seek to find a companion who can make us feel complete.

There is no place to look for such a companion other than within you. The place you start is the same as the place you end – the alpha and the omega are the same, as are the path and the goal. There is no room for effort from myself to me (the companion).

We keep putting off things that inspire us, make us happy, or were born to do. The rationale is that we will work hard now, no matter the type of work, and live our dreams later. In short, we follow the crowd and do what others do. That is what drives us, because that is how society works. We get entrenched in a forced pattern of living. It entraps us. It leaves us feeling drained and unhappy. To free ourselves, we try even harder. By doing the same things we have always done. Never having the courage to pause and reflect. Every aspect of our lives carefully and meticulously planned and executed. Despite all these efforts, we still live in fear. Never feeling fully empowered, and hoping these efforts will bear fruit in the future. After the heart attack I knew intuitively, deep in my very soul, that I had to stop wasting our time and conquer my dreams, now or never.

Page 153

I had to free myself from my past and put in the work to do the things I was passionate about and born to do. I could no longer afford to cling to some ideas about the future and become a bitter old person with heavy-laden shoulders. I wanted to start living now, feel empowered and fearless.

There is a difference between hearing and listening. We can listen with or without our heart. Listening with the intellect brings dichotomy – what is right/wrong, believable/ unbelievable, correct/incorrect. Our head will draw different meanings. We will be told one thing, we will hear another.

To listen with the heart, we must learn to be quiet. For that we must leave our intellect, and learn the art of being quiet. It requires what Zen masters call "no-mind", which Kabir names the *unmani* state. Buddha refers to it as the dissolution of the mind, and Patanjali named it *nirvilkala samadhi*, the samadhi without thoughts. A state in which all doubts and debates end, and where existence, sound and energy, all are one.

A lot of actions we carry out are based on pleasing others, saving grace, superstition, copying others, rituals from religion we were born into, or simply "It has always been done this way by our elders." They are just that – actions, providing little or no benefit. A tick-box exercise to keep us "happy and safe." Done that, no more guilt. Now, on to actions that really make us happy and satisfied. That is how our lives really work. A balancing act between meaningful and meaningless actions. Never living fully, and always wanting to be somewhere else, or doing something else.

I have, in the last 9 chapters, shared my inner secrets with you. There might be many things you might be ashamed of but, instead of being hard on yourself, bring forgiveness and reconciliation. Look around you, and take stock of the people who have always surrounded and supported you, even in your worst moments. These relationships are the doorways to seeing who you really are – they provide insights about the best and worst within you. Relationships can provide the wisdom and courage for change. They can awaken you from a state of slumber and to more conscious living. Relationships can show you the marvel of the inner beauty in all of us, and guide you to see the "one-ness", the "connectedness" of all that surrounds you. You cannot do this on your own. You need prayer, contemplation and guidance – let the one-ness find you – have faith. Relationships can guide, support and inspire us to live meaningful lives. So why lead life as if in a deep sleep? Waking up means living every moment committed to meaningful actions. A life of flourishing relationships and doing what matters most – puran hoye chitt ki Icha.

You are a beautiful person who has come bearing gifts for this amazing world. In your haste, don't forget to share them. Stop and contemplate on this.